GLOUCESTERSHIRE COU~~~

Headquarters : **BERKELEY HOUSE, GLOUCESTER.**

Tel. : Glos. 21444.

Open to the Public : Mon.—Fri., 9 a.m. to 5 p.m.
Sat., 9 a.m. to 12 noon.

NOTICE TO READERS.

The last date entered below is the date by which this book
must be returned.

Readers are requested to take care of the books while in
their possession and to point out any defect that they may
observe in them to the local Librarian.

Date of Return	Date of Return	Date of Return	Date of Return
23 MAY 1950	27 OCT 1954		
19 JUL 1950	5 - NOV 1954		
13 NOV 1950			
	23 SEP 1955		
2 NOV 1951	2 MAY 1956		
14 DEC 1951	23 JAN 1957		
25 MAR 1952	1 AUG 1957		
21 APR 1952	4. OCT. 1962		
3 MAY 1952			
30 MAR 1953			
22 AUG 1953			

GLOUCESTERSHIRE EDUCATION COMMITTEE.

THIS LABEL MUST NOT BE TORN OUT.

C.L. 16.   S 72544.

THE FAMILY HONOUR

THE FAMILY HONOUR (ACT IV)
A scene from the Glasgow Production, January 1947

THE FAMILY HONOUR

A Comedy of Four Acts
and an Epilogue

by

LAURENCE HOUSMAN

JONATHAN CAPE
THIRTY BEDFORD SQUARE
LONDON

FIRST PUBLISHED 1950

GLOUCESTERSHIRE COUNTY LIBRARY

CLASS 822

COPY C

PRINTED IN GREAT BRITAIN BY BUTLER AND TANNER LTD.
FROME AND LONDON
BOUND BY A. W. BAIN AND CO. LTD.

PREFACE

It may interest the readers of this Play to know that the main incident, round which it was written, actually happened to a far-distant relative of my own, a contemporary, and close connection by marriage, of my great-grandfather. But though the date, and the setting, and the circumstances were all very much as here given, the denouement was somewhat different. The situation presented possibilities too tempting for a dramatist to deny himself the opportunity of a moral improvement on what actually took place. And so, in my play, I have allowed myself to substitute poetic justice for villainy triumphant — which is what really happened. For, I am sorry to say, that my four-times-removed great-uncle (if that may be reckoned as our approximate relationship) succumbed tamely to the blackmailers, and accepted forced marriage, at the point of three pistols, to a lady who (herself innocent of the plot) became an excellent wife, and the mother and grandmother of two notable characters in the mid- and the late-Victorian age — the one a famous preacher and reciter, and the other a no less famous actor, better known in America than in this country.

To this Play, founded on fact, I have added an Epilogue, not intended primarily for stage performances. I wrote it because I hoped that some of my readers might share my interest in what happened afterwards to those four shady characters, the brothers of my heroine; and, especially as to what became of the prudent and calculating one — Jonathan. It was his end which most interested me, and which I wished to put on record, because it helped to tell what I thought of him.

And having done this, I feel that I must add something about one's choosing of names for characters in works of fiction. Sometimes — when one is inventing or discovering a character — a name imposes itself without the author having anything to do in the matter. And this is the second time that I have been obliged to give to one of my shady characters a name, toward a certain possessor of which I have good reason for feelings of friendship and respect. When I wrote the life of that rascal 'Mr. Trimblerigg', I found that I had to call him 'Jonathan': I apologized, and I was forgiven. And now, once more, I have felt obliged to give the same name to another, who was hardly better. I can only say, in extenuation, that I have, in this Play, given a variant of my own name to the worst character of them all.

LAURENCE HOUSMAN

ACKNOWLEDGMENT

THE frontispiece is reproduced by kind permission of the Glasgow Citizens' Theatre, Ltd., from a photograph by T. & R. Annan, Glasgow.

6

CHARACTERS

JAMES BURKLYNCH (an Irish Landowner)

LARRY
JONATHAN
BRIAN } (his sons)
RORY

HONOR (his daughter)

BRIDGET (a maid-servant)

JOHN DURHAM (an Englishman)

7

The Family Honour was first produced on 26 January 1948 by the Glasgow Citizens' Theatre with the following cast:

JAMES BURKLYNCH	LAURENCE HARDY
HONOR (his daughter)	LENNOX MILNE
JONATHAN ⎫	DENNIS CANNAN
LARRY ⎪ (his sons)	PETER MACDONNELL
BRIAN ⎬	ANDREW KEIR
RORY ⎭	DANIEL THORNDIKE
BRIDGET	MARY WALTON
JOHN DURHAM	KENNETH MACKINTOSH

PRODUCED BY JOHN CASSON

ACT I

ACT I

In a remote part of North Ireland, in or about the year 1829, and (to come nearer to the point) in the best bedroom of the old and rather decayed home of an old and rather decayed family of Irish gentry, the master of the house sits waiting for death. About that he has no uncertainty, nor any qualms of conscience; but his acceptance of the inevitable is not of a religious character. Being of rigid Protestant persuasion, he has no use for a priest; and though one of his sons has taken orders in the Established Church, he has no use for him either. He is just dying as an Irish gentleman should, much as he has lived, without any special repentance for the past, and without expecting any special favour for his future in the world to come. The only person he has any use for (or affection) is his daughter HONOR, *who is now attending on him, a strong upstanding woman — not middle-aged yet, though past her first youth. She moves quietly and competently; and, when she speaks, it is to the point, as one who knows her mind, and will stick to it.*

The room is sparely furnished with large pieces which have seen their best days. The double-bed, topped by a canopy with dull faded hangings, stands central; but the very mortal man, who should now be its occupant, sits in a high-backed armchair between bed and window, half-dressed in shirt and breeches, and an old dressing-gown of once-rich material. This is JAMES BURKLYNCH, *landed proprietor, aged seventy, widower, and father of a surviving family of four sons, and one daughter. His daughter has just given him his medicine; he drinks it, and hands back the glass.*

BURKLYNCH There! I only take it to let you have your way, and be left in peace. But no good will it do me — no good at all.

HONOR It's good for you to obey doctor's orders, Father.

BURKLYNCH *Your* orders, Honor. It's no so often he comes to trouble me now.

HONOR Seeing, maybe, he thinks you're getting better.

BURKLYNCH You know I'm not that; nor ever shall be again. No ... more likely as being doubtful whether he'll ever get paid for it — if he did come — when I'm gone.

HONOR I'd see he was paid, Father.

BURKLYNCH How would you? Your brothers wouldn't; and the purse-strings won't be in your keeping — not if they know it.

HONOR Oh, there's ways and ways, when you've got a will of your own. And whatever happens, they couldn't well do without me — could they now?

BURKLYNCH They've never tried — yet.

HONOR Let them!

BURKLYNCH Aye! And that reminds me of something I've got to do — before I go. You find them for me.

HONOR Find what?

BURKLYNCH Wasn't it of your brothers I was speaking?

HONOR Which of them do you want?

BURKLYNCH All of 'em. Where are they?

HONOR It 'ud be hard to say where *all* of 'em are, Father — any time of the day — or night either.

BURKLYNCH Aye: *or* night. You know 'em well, don't you? But they shouldn't be far out of call just now — me being as I am. You go find them, Honor, and send them to me.

HONOR I wish you'd let me put you to bed first, Father. You'd be more comfortable there.

BURKLYNCH If I took to my bed now, 'twould be the end of me: I'd never get up again.

HONOR. Is that why you've stayed out of it so long? It's not been good for you.

BURKLYNCH Whatever's the quickest way is what's good for me now. And sitting-up I can think better; and it's now I've got to — a bit late, maybe. You go and call 'em, and tell 'em — nothing: except they'd better be quick. Aye, tell 'em that!

> (*She goes. He watches till she has closed the door, then gets up very painfully and slowly; his hand goes to his heart; he halts, mutters* 'Go slow! Go slow!' *then, holding on to the bed-rail, crosses to the chest of drawers, pulls out the top drawer, fumbles in it, and takes out a paper. He returns slowly to his chair, again holding on by the bed-rail, and is just about to sit down again when* HONOR *returns*)

HONOR Father! What have you got up for?

BURKLYNCH (*with grim satisfaction*) Ah! I've done it: had my feet under me again without any to help me. I just wanted to see . . . You found 'em?

HONOR I found Jonathan. I've sent him to find the others.

BURKLYNCH Oh! Jonathan? So he's come, has he? How is his Reverence?

HONOR. He's himself all right. He asked how you were, Father.

BURKLYNCH (*drily*) Oh? Very decent and dutiful that was.

HONOR And his lordship sends you a brace of pheasants with his kind compliments.

BURKLYNCH Ah! Very good of his lordship to remember poor relatives — such as we; though, maybe, they come too late for me to have the tasting of 'em.

HONOR You shall have them today, Father. Now,

13

sit you back, and be comfortable. (*She arranges the cushions.*) And no more talking, mind! You've talked enough for the while.

BURKLYNCH Nay, I've got to talk now; I've been putting it off too long. . . . I wish I could have got you married, Honor, before I went. You've had a hard life of it, with all to look after since your mother died. Ten years it is; and you're not so young now for it to be easy to make a match for you. I ought to have seen to it before, but I couldn't spare you: selfish of me that was; I'm like the rest.

HONOR Oh, that's all right, Father. There's no man come along yet that I've wanted to marry.

BURKLYNCH Is that true?

HONOR It is: none, anyway, that I've had more than a passing fancy for — as is only natural. For when a maid sees a decent well-set-up man, maybe she'll be thinking what fine children they might have if they made a match of it. But the thought of it goes when he goes: it means nothing.

BURKLYNCH But you'd like to marry some day, Honor, wouldn't you?

HONOR Yes. I'd like to have a man of my own, and children of my own; to do my best for 'em all. That's what a woman's life's for, I reckon. As it is, I've had you, Father (I don't complain of that) and four brothers as don't belong to me so much as I belong to them: only three, now that Jonathan's gone to be chaplain to his lordship.

BURKLYNCH You don't want that to go on?

HONOR No, Father, I don't want that to go on.

BURKLYNCH Well, I'll do my best for you.

(*The door opens.* JONATHAN *enters in clerical attire*)

HONOR Ah, here's Jonathan.

14

JONATHAN Well, Father! How are you finding yourself today? Better?

BURKLYNCH Aye, better it is, for what's got to be. Time and I, we be parting by like ways — from a day that's shortening to a night that's going to be longer. So your Reverence has come over to see your father make his mark — 'finished' — to a life that might have been better. But I'll no be asking *your* blessing, Jonathan; 'twouldn't count, I reckon. How's his lordship?

JONATHAN Oh, much as usual; very regular in his habits, such as they are — under the table most nights when dinner is over; and in his bed next day till noon's gone, without knowing how he got there. And full of inventing new cures for the old complaint. He's good at that, though they haven't cured it for him — so far.

BURKLYNCH And when d'you say his prayers for him?

JONATHAN Says 'em himself; doesn't trouble me with 'em. It does not take him long either; but he means it; so there's hope that Heaven hears him and'll give a satisfactory answer. And a good prayer it is: 'To Hell with the Pope and all them that worship graven images!' I say it myself, in other words, when I have to do the preaching.

BURKLYNCH Now to think that I've got a son in the Church, and I've never heard him preach! What a missed opportunity was that! And when you preach my funeral sermon, I'll no have the pleasure to hear that either.

JONATHAN 'Twill be more pleasant for you to hear, maybe, that his lordship has sent you a brace of pheasants with kind inquiries how you're finding yourself.

BURKLYNCH Remember to thank him for me, and say I'll do my best to have a taste of them before I go. . . . Now where are the rest of you? Did you not find them?

JONATHAN I found them for you, Father. They said they'd be coming along soon. And here they are.

(*Enter the three other members of the Burklynch family*, LARRY, BRIAN, RORY. *They are strong, healthy-looking specimens, careless and somewhat slovenly in their attire. As they enter, each in turn gives his parent the perfunctory greeting of* 'Hullo, Father'; RORY *coming last, adds* 'Feeling better?' *The old man eyes them sourly, and grunts*)

BURKLYNCH You haven't been in a great hurry to come, have you? Maybe you guessed 'twas for something that's not going to please you. . . . Honor, now your brothers have come, you can go. I'll not need you till I've finished with them.

HONOR If it's more talking there's got to be, don't you be long, Father.

BURKLYNCH It depends on them how long I've got to be. They are a slow lot; getting a new idea into their heads takes time.

HONOR Ah, now don't tire yourself on *them*, Father; it'll not pay you.

(*She gives them a nod of understanding, as she goes out*)

BURKLYNCH You heard that? Tiring myself over *you* has never paid *me* anything.

LARRY And when have you ever paid us anything for what we've done for you, Father?

BURKLYNCH And what have you done?

LARRY Haven't we looked after the land for you?

BURKLYNCH You've looked *at* it; and watched others at work on it; and ridden over the crops for a short cut

16

on your way to hounds. But since I got past seeing to it, the land's gone poor, ye've so starved it.

RORY It always was poor; and there's no getting it better.

BURKLYNCH And another thing: since you took over, the men haven't worked as they did under me. You've slacked; so they've slacked. You've bred a good horse or two — I'll say that for you; and they've won races for those you sold them to — which they wouldn't have done, maybe, if you had had the training of them yourselves.

BRIAN Maybe they *would*; but training costs a devil of a lot these days, and takes time; and we hadn't the money for it.

BURKLYNCH No: and it's money I've got to talk to you about — what you're waiting to get when I'm gone. You are not to have it; it's to be for Honor.

LARRY Honor? What'll *she* want with it?

BURKLYNCH To get married.

LARRY But we don't want Honor married.

BURKLYNCH No; I can just fancy you don't! Where'd you be without Honor to do for you? And where'd I have been if I'd only had *you*.

RORY We've always tried to be kind to you, Father.

BRIAN And we've always had a respect for you.

LARRY Times — we may have been a bit thoughtless, being young; for which — yourself being old — you did not make allowances enough.

BURKLYNCH Allowances! You made your own allowances, and never worked for 'em. Was there one of you I could ever trust when my back was turned? If I'd left you to pay the wages, would I be sure you'd done it without keeping some of it back for yourselves?

LARRY You never caught me doing *that*, Father.

BURKLYNCH No, I didn't; but you might have done it, for all that.

LARRY Now, if any man but my father said that to me, I should call him out.

BURKLYNCH And shoot him for telling you the truth, eh? And that's what you call honour!

JONATHAN All this is very painful, and uncalled for, Father. Would you not wish to be making your end in charity with all men? And surely with your sons no less than others.

BURKLYNCH There speaks his Reverence! So you're setting God on to me now, are you? What sort of a God was it that let me beget sons like you — not knowing what I was doing?

BRIAN Oh, you knew what you were doing, Father!

BURKLYNCH Not what was to come of it, I didn't. Had I known *that* — well! I know what I'm doing now. You are not going to get rid of me, till I've had a promise from all of you that you'll do right by Honor when I'm gone.

RORY Oh, we'll always keep Honor; we're not for turning her out, Father.

BURKLYNCH You are 'not for turning her out'. Now that's a good joke, that is! Did you mean it? Well, *I am*! I am for turning her out into the hands of an honest man who'll know the worth of her, and have respect for her, and'll work to give her a decent living, which you'd never do. When the mortgage is paid off — ye'll have twelve months allowed you to do it in — there'll be four or five hundred left over; and I'll have you promise that you'll see Honor married before any of you touch a penny of it.

BRIAN You mean it's to be for Honor?

BURKLYNCH It's to be for Honor.

LARRY *All* of it?

BURKLYNCH Yes, all of it, if she needs it for getting the right husband such as she deserves.

BRIAN There was not any such condition, Father,

18

when we agreed to break the entail, so the money could be raised.

BURKLYNCH No; and it wasn't a condition either that Honor should give the best ten years of her life to look after you, while you were all growing up to a life of idleness — a devil-may-care lot, and a by-word to all the county. So I'll have Honor married to get her away from you. You'd all live on her, wouldn't you? — if she gave you the chance — taking your ease, and she slaving to her life's end. Which of you has ever done an honest day's work, for yourself or anybody? Jonathan went into the Church, hoping to get the family living. Well, being in his lordship's gift, maybe he'll give it him when it falls vacant; so he's provided for. Brian thinks he'd like to emigrate to America. He might do worse. Maybe he'll learn in a new country what the old country's never taught him — to work. So there'll be two of you left. Well, when the mortgage comes to be paid off, and the estate has to be sold, the new owner may take you as his tenants — or maybe not. Anyway you'll have a year to turn round in before you have to turn out. And between now and then you've got to get Honor married, on what remains over from the sale, before you touch a penny of it — to a good man, one that she'll consent to; not just one that would be willing to take her for the price of a bottle of whisky, which is all the care you'd have about it.

BRIAN It's to be for her dower, you mean, Father?

BURKLYNCH Yes: if you can't get her married otherwise. If you could hit on a man with sense enough, he'd ask no dower to get one like *her*.

RORY Aye: she's good in the house; but she's not the marrying kind.

BURKLYNCH Who says?

RORY Has any man ever come along and asked for her?

BURKLYNCH Yes; one did; and I turned him off. She never knew of it. That's what I did; it's been on my mind; and I've got to make up for it.

LARRY Ah, now, don't excite yourself, Father. We'll see Honor married.

BURKLYNCH Aye, it's easy for you to say it; but saying is not enough. I'll have you write it and sign it, here and now. This is my will; (*he holds up the paper*) and it's to go along with it. Jonathan, take a seat at yon table, and write as I tell you.

LARRY Oh, Father, it's not necessary; and it's not to the honour of the family that you should be doubting us.

BURKLYNCH It's for me to decide what's necessary, not you. And I'll have Honor to know it, and have the writing of it in her own keeping. Sit down, and write, Jonathan.

(JONATHAN *sits down at the table, takes up a pen, and opens the inkstand*)

JONATHAN There's no ink here, Father; it's all dried up.

BURKLYNCH What for are you making so much trouble? Put water in it, or fetch more. Be quick now.

(*Exit* JONATHAN)

BRIAN I think, Father, you should have given us more notice of this.

BURKLYNCH What for?

BRIAN So that we might consult with each other. It's a serious matter if we are not to have our shares in what the breaking of the entail was to bring — which you could not have done, had you not got our consent to it.

BURKLYNCH The entail had to be broken because

20

you'd got me into such debt with your misdoings that there was no other way out of it.

RORY Oh, we'd three years of bad luck, that was all, Father.

BURKLYNCH Three years? 'Twas my twenty-three years of bad luck with you and the rest that did the mischief. And what use have you made of the five years that have gone since — not bad years any of 'em — after we were able to raise the mortgage. How much of that money did you put on to the land? You still went on running into debts, which I had to pay for you.

LARRY They were debts of honour, Father. You wouldn't have had us *not* pay them?

BURKLYNCH Debts of honour! Where's the honour, when you lay wagers, and haven't the money to pay up when you lose? You would always be telling me then how you'd agreed for the money to be raised for the benefit of all of you. So I let you have it, when I should have made you sell your horses, and go on foot for a while, till you could afford to ride honestly again, out of your own earnings.

LARRY Oh, you can't have the gentry to be seen walking, Father — not in Ireland; and we that are known to be related to his lordship.

BURKLYNCH Aye, related — distantly. But even that's not going to get you wives from any of the gentry of this county where you are known. No man in his senses would let one of his daughters marry into this family. . . . I'll have no more words!

(*Meanwhile*, JONATHAN *has returned with the ink*)

Sit down, Jonathan, and write *this* . . . 'We, the undersigned, do hereby promise and confirm that until our sister Honor be married, as she shall be free to choose, we will take no share to ourselves of any moneys that do come to us after our Father's demise; and that any dower that may be necessary for our said sister's marriage, shall be a first charge on the estate when sold. . . . Given under our hands this' . . . What date is the day?

RORY November the . . . fourteenth is it not?

LARRY No: it's the thirteenth.

RORY Ah, well! make it the fourteenth then, which is better: the thirteenth would be bringing us bad luck, maybe — and this a Friday.

BURKLYNCH Now sign, all of you. Larry, you are the eldest. (LARRY *signs*) Now then, you, Jonathan. (JONATHAN *signs*) Now you, Rory. (RORY *signs*) Now then, Brian. Where are you? Come on!

BRIAN I'm not ready for it yet. I'll sign tomorrow maybe; when I've thought more about it.

BURKLYNCH There's nothing to think about, that needs waiting till tomorrow. You sign it now.

BRIAN But there is, Father. You agreed that I should go to America; but I cannot go if I have not the money for it. I must talk to Honor first. I'll go and see her now; and if she's reasonable about it, there'll be no need for me to sign at all.

BURKLYNCH You'll no see Honor; I forbid you to see Honor; *I'm* going to see Honor.

BRIAN I'll bring her to you, Father. But I'll be seeing her first.

(*He goes*)

BURKLYNCH Jonathan, go and fetch Honor; tell her she's to come here to me, *now*.

(JONATHAN *goes*)

And, Rory, you bring me that paper, so I have it safe in my own hands.

(RORY *brings it*)

22

Well? What do you think about it now? Are you wishing *you* hadn't signed?

LARRY I don't mind myself having signed, Father; but I think Brian was right.

BURKLYNCH Oh? You think Brian was right. And what about you, Rory?

RORY I don't think he was wrong, Father: he had his reasons. How'll he get to America if he hasn't the money?

(JONATHAN *returns, followed by* HONOR)

BURKLYNCH He can work for it here — same as the rest of you. There's no need for him to go to America till Honor's married.

JONATHAN Here's Honor, Father.

BURKLYNCH Then now you can all go. Leave Honor to me.

(*They go*)

HONOR Will I bring you your broth, Father? You will be needing it, after so much talking. Oh! and it's been bad for you.

BURKLYNCH I'll have it presently. Has Brian been trying to talk to you?

HONOR He was just beginning, Father, when Jonathan came to fetch me.

BURKLYNCH You're not to let him. Honor, you keep this. (*He gives her the paper*) Three of them have signed it, and Brian's *going* to sign it. It's to get you married.

HONOR Oh, Father, surely I can see to that for myself?

BURKLYNCH You cannot: not these days — and the Burklynch name being what it is — what my sons have made it — not without you have a dower. Put it into yonder drawer, that has a key to it; lock it, and see that you keep it safe, when I'm gone.

23

*(HONOR puts it in the drawer and locks it. Outside
two pistol-shots are heard, followed by raised
voices and laughter)*

What's that noise?

*(HONOR goes to the window, and looks out. Two
more shots follow)*

What is it?

HONOR It's Larry and Brian practising with their
pistols at a target.

BURKLYNCH What will they be doing that for?

HONOR Oh, it's just what's come into their heads,
having nothing else to do. It's the way they have. It's
to get their hands in for the next duel they'll be fighting,
maybe.

BURKLYNCH Tell them they're to stop it.

*(HONOR opens the window. Two more shots are
heard: and BRIAN's voice: 'I am beating you,
Larry!')*

HONOR Brian! Larry! Stop that noise!

LARRY Aye, presently! We've got a wager on; and
we've got to finish. Two more. 'Twill be soon over!

BURKLYNCH Soon over! Here am I a dying man,
and my sons shooting at a target to pass the time till
I'm gone. My God! let me get my last word to them
now!

*(He gets to his feet, and staggers toward the win-
dow. Suddenly he stops. His hand goes to his
heart)*

HONOR Oh, Father! Father! come back, and lay
yourself down!

(She helps him to the bed)

24

Put up your feet! and lay your head down! and keep still, oh! keep still!

> (*He lies gasping for breath. She runs to the window*)

Larry! Larry! Ride for the doctor, quick!

> (*As the* CURTAIN *descends, she runs back to the bed, to apply remedies which will be of no use — no use at all*)

ACT II

ACT II

Twelve months have passed since the old man's death,
which took place a few minutes after the fall of the curtain
in Act I.

It is evening: and in the family living-room (with its
old-fashioned furniture, which has long since seen its best
days) HONOR *and* BRIDGET, *the maid, are clearing the sup-*
per table. Some of the chairs have been drawn away from
the table, and are grouped about the hearth, on which a peat
and log fire is burning

HONOR Well! nothing wrong with their appetites,
seemingly; they haven't left much! But you can take
that with you to your mother when you go, Bridget.

(*She gives* BRIDGET *the remains of a pie*)

BRIDGET Thank you, Miss Honor.

HONOR How is she?

BRIDGET Better, Miss Honor, and hoping soon to be
back at work. But it still needs someone to put her to
bed, and get her up in the morning. She can't well do
it herself.

HONOR Well, so long as you can be here most of the
day, I can get along without you for the rest. . . . There,
you can take out the tray.

(BRIDGET *takes up the tray, goes to the door, stops,*
and turns back)

What's the matter?

BRIDGET It's Mr. Larry, Miss Honor.

HONOR Well? What about him?

BRIDGET He did that to me today, which he didn't
ought to have done.

HONOR Did what?

BRIDGET Took hard hold of me, and kissed me.

HONOR Kissed you, did he? Well, next time he does it, slap him — hard. I give you leave.

BRIDGET Oh! I couldn't take such a liberty, Miss Honor!

HONOR Then it's not a liberty; it's an order. You do it, and say Miss Honor told you to — so he'll learn better.

BRIDGET I can't do it with this in my hands, Miss Honor. . . . He's out there waiting.

HONOR Give it here, then! (*She takes the tray*) Now you go. And let me hear you do it, mind!

(BRIDGET *goes;* HONOR *stands listening; presently a resounding slap is heard.* HONOR *gives a nod of satisfaction, sets down the tray, goes to the door, and calls:*)

Larry! Larry! . . . Come here; I want you.

(LARRY *enters, trying to look innocent*)

What were you doing?

LARRY Nothing.

HONOR Don't lie! You've been trying to kiss Bridget, and getting yourself smacked for it.

LARRY How did you know?

HONOR I heard it; and she's left her mark on your face. Serve you right! Now just you let Bridget alone! It's because of you, and the rest that her mother won't have her stay in the house for the night. She's an honest girl; she's got her own man waiting to marry her.

LARRY I've done her no harm.

HONOR No; but you want to . . . Bridget, come back and fetch out this tray. (BRIDGET *returns*) It's all right, Bridget. Mr. Larry is waiting to make you his apologies.

30

(Thus morally compelled, LARRY, *somewhat sullenly, does as required)*

LARRY I'm sorry, Bridget.

BRIDGET Oh, it's no matter, Mr. Larry — leastways, not all that much — to need talking about. I hope I didn't hurt you. It was only at Miss Honor's orders I did it.

HONOR Now, Bridget, don't *you* go apologizing! Off with you!

*(*BRIDGET *takes the tray, and goes)*

Larry, I want some money. There's a lot of bills owing, waiting to be paid.

LARRY Well, owe 'em, and let 'em wait! Aren't we well enough known around the country, for folk to be willing to bide till it's convenient for us to pay 'em?

HONOR Yes, we are! Which is why the wise ones are beginning to ask for their money.

LARRY Well, I haven't got any.

HONOR You've got what you sold the old horse for to Mr. O'Donovan, a week ago.

LARRY He hasn't paid up yet.

HONOR Yes, he has. When he came yesterday to fetch him away, I asked him, and he said 'Yes.'

LARRY 'Twas not for you to be interfering in such a matter. It's a real caution you are, Honor!

HONOR I need to be. And there's something else I happen to know. Now that the mortgage has been paid off from what the estate has fetched, there'll be something over. Well, in a year's time, unless you take on the land as tenants to the new owner, we'll have to quit. Meanwhile we've got to live somehow; and I need money for the housekeeping, and the week's wages. How much'll it be?

LARRY How much what?

HONOR How much will there be left over from the paying off of the mortgage?

LARRY Not much.

HONOR I daresay. I said 'How much?'

LARRY Oh, just a few hundred, maybe: more or less.

HONOR Aye: maybe a bit more than you'd like me to know. Well, I suppose you think you can live on that for another year or two, just waiting for something else to turn up: which it won't. *I'll* not be for that, Larry.

LARRY (*startled*) What do you mean?

HONOR If we can't pay our way honestly, I'll go out to service, and earn my own living.

LARRY Oh! you wouldn't do us *that* disgrace, Honor! And we of the gentry!

HONOR I would! I'm not asking you to get me married — I haven't seen the man I'd wish for it yet. Maybe I never shall. But you've got to put that money you signed about in my keeping — just in case it *should* be wanted.

LARRY How will it be wanted?

HONOR (*drily*) For my dower, if you can't get rid of me without paying for it.

LARRY (*defensively*) We didn't *all* sign, Honor.

HONOR No; you didn't. And if you like to let Brian stay out of it, and keep his share to himself, you can do it.

LARRY Oh, we wouldn't like him to do that at all.

HONOR Well, tell him so.

LARRY But, Honor, if you are not for marrying, what use will the money be, while it's there waiting?

HONOR It'll have this use, Larry: it won't be spent; it'll be in safe keeping.

LARRY But I think what our Father meant was that you should get married at once. And if you don't marry at all, you've no right to it.

32

HONOR My right can wait; and so can yours. I'm in no hurry. If I don't marry in three years, you shall have it all back. There's a fair offer.

LARRY Three years is a long time, Honor.

HONOR Long enough, maybe, to make you find work to get your living by. If it does that, it'll be doing you a real kindness.

LARRY I will see what the others have to say about it.

HONOR Aye, do. I daresay they won't like it, any better than you do . . .

(And just then in come BRIAN, RORY *and* JON-ATHAN*)*

Ah, here they are. You've come just when you are wanted. Larry's got to have a talk with you.

(She starts to go with the remains of the clearing; then puts her head in again to say)

And it's not to be only *talk*, mind you!

(She has gone)

RORY What's it all about?

LARRY *(sourly)* Honor knows.

RORY Knows what?

LARRY That there'll be something left over after the paying off of the mortgage.

BRIAN How did she get to know that?

LARRY It must have been the damned lawyer that told her. And a breach of professional etiquette, it was, to tell anything — to one that wasn't his client.

JONATHAN She's one of the family though; you can't leave that out.

LARRY She didn't have anything to do with the signing of the deed for the breaking of the entail: 'twas only heirs male had that right.

JONATHAN Well, what does she say about it?

LARRY She's been very exorbitant and interfering. Says she must have the money in her own keeping, while she decides whether she'll marry, or no. And I tell her that if we are ready and willing to marry her to anyone she chooses, and she doesn't accept, the money's not hers. She's no right to keep it, if there's any doubt about it ever being wanted.

RORY But what use will the money be to us, if it has to go to get her married now?

LARRY Oh, we must find somebody who'll be willing to marry into the gentry, without asking for a dower, or not more than we can spare of it.

JONATHAN Are you not forgetting that, if necessary, she's due to have all of it?

LARRY She can't! It's not reasonable!

JONATHAN It's what we promised the old man, and put our names to. I wrote it as he told me: I could say you the words of it.

RORY Eh! He was not in his right mind to be asking for such a promise: nor were we in our right minds when we made it. So it's not binding.

LARRY And mind you, all we promised was to get her married: the money was only to help, if we couldn't do it otherwise.

RORY Then we must find the man.

BRIAN And where will you find him?

RORY Oh, there must be many lying about in the world — some widower, maybe, with children needing to be looked after. We've only got to hit on the right man, and tell him what's waiting for him. For Honor — she's a good housekeeper; I'll say that for her.

BRIAN How'll you get him?

RORY Advertise in the county paper: 'Widower wanted for a good housekeeper to look after him. Money no consideration, so long as of good standing

34

and character.' Anyone that knew Honor, and had the good sense for it, would pay money to get her.

BRIAN Well, you might try! Invite all the widowers of the county to come and meet her.

RORY Aye! Sure, and why not? And let her go to the highest bidder.

LARRY Ah, you've the hopeful mind, Rory!

RORY It's the only way to get through the world, if you haven't the means to do it otherwise.

LARRY Aye, and a good enough way if wishes were horses; which they aren't. And talking of horses, here's Honor wanting me to hand over to her what I got from O'Donovan last week for old Dobbin.

BRIAN What for?

LARRY Oh, for the housekeeping, and the wages! Did you ever? Who was she thinking it belonged to, to be asking for it like that? I told her what I thought of her.

BRIAN Now I didn't know that you'd got the money, Larry. You'll remember that you are owing me something on that last bet we had together that you lost.

LARRY Aye, you shall have it presently.

BRIAN Well, so long as it's before Honor gets hold of it. A caution she is!

LARRY Which is what I told her.

(*He gets up to stir the fire. As he does so, loud knocking is heard at the outer door*)

RORY Now whoever will that be, this time o' night? Which of us would you have go and see?

BRIAN You, Rory, as you are the hopeful one. Maybe it's one of the widowers come to ask for Honor before you've advertised for him.

RORY Ah, well, it *might* be.

(*He goes out;* BRIAN *calls after him*)

35

BRIAN Ask him 'Are you a widower?' And if he isn't, shut the door on him!

> (*They sit and listen. The opening and shutting of the house-door is heard, followed by the sound of voices, and presently footsteps approaching*)

LARRY Aye: he's let him in . . . I don't know that voice: it sounds like a stranger.

> (RORY *returns, accompanied by the stranger, who is presently to be known as* MR. JOHN DURHAM. *He is a tall well-set-up man, youngish, in the late twenties; from his manner obviously a gentleman, and from his accent an Englishman*)

RORY Come in, and sit down, and warm yourself. You need be in no hurry to be getting along further.

DURHAM Thank you! Thank you! (*Then, bowing to the company*) Your servant, Gentlemen.

LARRY Yours, sir. We are happy to meet you.

DURHAM I am sorry, indeed, to be troubling you at such an hour; but in this country, which is strange to me, I have lost my way. Can you direct me to an inn, or any place where I can put up for the night?

LARRY My good sir, there is no inn round here less than three good miles away, and that but a poor one.

DURHAM Well, if you will kindly direct me; and — to ask a great favour — if you would allow me to stable my horse here for the night: for just now he had a fall, and has hurt himself, I fear.

LARRY Why, surely we will! And as for going further yourself, you are not to think of it! We'll put you up here for the night — the two of you.

DURHAM That is a most kind offer. But I hardly like to presume on your good willingness.

LARRY No: it's a pleasure, and a great satisfaction to be of service to a gentleman such as yourself, which I see you are: and your horse too. We are great lovers of horses in this country. He's had a fall, you say? And I see, by your coat, that you've shared it. I'll go straight away now, and see after him.

DURHAM That is a kindly thought, sir. But you must allow me to come with you.

LARRY Aye, come with me, and introduce me to the gentleman. And maybe you'd be glad to have a meal, when we come back in again?

DURHAM Indeed, I should, sir. For it is several hours since I stayed by the way to have anything.

LARRY Come on, then! . . . Rory, go and tell Honor that we've got a visitor that will be staying the night. . . . And your horse has hurt himself, you say? Is it badly, do you think?

DURHAM I think not; I hope not.

(*They go out, talking as they go.* RORY *moves toward the door, then halts to say:*)

RORY Well? What do you think of him?

BRIAN Oh, he looks well enough — for an Englishman; which is what, by his speech, I take him to be. But not old enough yet to be a widower, Rory. Why did you let him in?

RORY (*playing up*) Oh, but there's no knowing! And where's the harm? If we find we don't want him, we can send him off in the morning.

(*He goes to the door, puts his head out, and calls:*)

Honor! . . . Honor!

(HONOR *comes hurrying in*)

HONOR What is it? Who is it, that has come?

JONATHAN Who he is, we don't yet rightly know, Honor. But he looks decent: just a stranger that has lost his way.

37

BRIAN And he wants a meal, and a bed for the night, and a stable for his horse, which Larry and he have just gone to see after.

HONOR Oh, then, to be sure, it's right; and we will make him welcome. I'll see what I can do, though there's nothing left over from supper. I gave Bridget the last bit of pie to take home with her; and she's gone now. But there's the ham, and there's cheese; and I can do a scramble of eggs for him.

BRIAN Oh, that'll do all right; and if he feels he wants anything more he must fill up with the whisky.

JONATHAN But where will you put him to sleep, Honor, now I'm here?

HONOR There's only one room where we can put him, unless he's to share a bed with one of you — the one Father died in, though it's not been used since. It's the best we can do. (*As she talks she starts laying the table*) But so late it is now, you'll have to keep him up talking an hour or more, while I get things ready, and the bed aired and all. And no fire laid, either; and I doubt whether it would be safe to light one, for the chimney has never been swept, and so damp that it 'ud sure to smoke down into the room. And there's that old jackdaw's nest up in the top, that I told you to get cleared away, Rory, but you never did.

RORY Ah, he can do without a fire: a warming-pan to his bed will be all he needs.

HONOR Anyway, I'll have more to do between now and then, than I'll be able to get through without someone to help me. Rory, make yourself useful, and come and fetch in some of the things.

(*She goes out quickly;* RORY *follows with little haste or willingness, and returns presently, with a tray which he unloads carelessly on to the table, leaving it for* HONOR *to arrange better*)

38

BRIAN Well, Jonathan, we didn't expect to have a visitor to meet you, when you came over for the night to talk business.

JONATHAN No, we don't often run to visitors, do we? And very pleasant it is that it should so happen. And he looks to me to be a man of good standing, with his fine manners; and his coat (which must have got itself torn in his fall — did you see?) is of the best make, and looks to be in the latest London fashion.

BRIAN I wonder what brings him here?

JONATHAN We'll be hearing, maybe, presently.

BRIAN Well, seeing you've let him in, have you made any plans about him, Rory?

RORY No; I was only just thinking that if the gentleman is not married we might ask him to stay on a bit; or to come later, and pay us a longer visit. It's just a chance; and it's only fair that we should be taking advantage of the kindness we are doing him: so he could not well refuse.

JONATHAN But what chance do you think there would be, Rory? I wouldn't wonder, from the look of him, if he wasn't a very well-off gentleman. And Honor is not so young and attractive as she was six years ago.

BRIAN No, she's not; and I haven't Rory's hopes about it. But there's other ways of attracting a man into marriage besides looks.

JONATHAN Aye: money. How's that going to help us?

BRIAN No, it will not; what I'm thinking now is of a way to save it for you. And mind you, it does not concern *me*: I didn't sign with the rest of you that Honor should have it; so my share stays mine whatever happens to yours and the others.

RORY But you wouldn't be taking advantage of that, Brian, over the rest of us, and call yourself a brother!

BRIAN I would. If I can't get to America without —

as Father promised that I should, when the entail was broken — I will just have to say that Father's promise to me came before your promise to Honor; and that I mean to have it.

JONATHAN Ah! you've the Scotsman in you, Brian.

BRIAN Aye; and maybe that's what's made me think of a way how you might save your money, and get Honor married (and a good match too, it might be) without having to find a dower for her.

JONATHAN Now how would you do that?

BRIAN Well, I'll tell you later, if it turns out that the man is eligible — bachelor, or widower. And if it works, I wouldn't wonder but we'll have it fixed no later than tomorrow morning before he goes.

RORY If you can do that Brian, you'll *be* a wonder.

BRIAN All it needs is a brain (which, so happens, is only another way of spelling 'Brian') and just a bit of quiet manipulation in the dark hours. When he comes in for his food, have it in your mind to ply him well with the whisky. He's only got an English head, that won't stand it as ours can.

RORY Ah! well, of course, that's only proper hospitality.

BRIAN I wonder, now, has he ever fought a duel? They don't run to duels much in England nowadays, the law being so much against it. But here in Ireland, praise be to God, the law has less to say about it.

JONATHAN You are talking riddles, Brian. What are you after?

BRIAN You shall have the answer when we've sent him to his bed, full of whisky. And you'll be grateful to me then; and you won't be grudging me my share when you get your own saved for you.

JONATHAN Well, as that touches the business I came over for, we'd better be talking about it; for with this stranger here, we may get no better chance later. How much will it be, what's over from the paying off of the mortgage?

BRIAN Five hundred pounds is what the lawyer tells us it'll be. Divided among four, you can't spare much of that for Honor.

JONATHAN We might get Honor married on a hundred, and share the rest equally.

BRIAN Aye: so long as a hundred-and-twenty-five remains *my* share. If Honor's to have a share, it's only to follow after mine.

JONATHAN I wouldn't have thought it of you, Brian.

BRIAN Who are *you* to be talking? Here's the family living coming to you, with three hundred a year sure and certain, and a good house to marry into as well.

JONATHAN Which is going to cost a lot for the furnishing of it. And, mind you, I haven't got more than the half-promise of it yet, from his lordship.

BRIAN He has no one else to give it to. And as for the furniture, you can take your share out of what's here when we quit.

JONATHAN And when's that going to be?

BRIAN It's got to be within a year, unless Larry and Rory make up their minds to stay on the land as tenants.

RORY What's the good of talking like that? We'll never make it pay, which is what it hasn't done these last five years and more.

BRIAN Well, then you'd better both come with me to America. If we put our money together, the three of us, we'd be able to make it go further, I shouldn't wonder.

RORY Aye, further *and* sooner. Your proposal doesn't attract me, Brian.

(*Re-enter* LARRY *and* MR. DURHAM)

LARRY He'll be all right now. You'll be able to ride

him tomorrow. Maybe you'd like to go and have a last look at him before we go to bed.

DURHAM Yes, if it won't be troubling you too much, I would; for we are great friends, he and I.

LARRY He's a fine horse. Have you had him long?

DURHAM Five years.

LARRY You must have paid a big price for him.

DURHAM Considering his quality, I got him very cheaply.

LARRY And you brought him over from England with you?

DURHAM I did. I was planning to make a tour of the country, and I thought the pleasantest way of doing it was by riding my own horse. So, here we are, the two of us.

LARRY And what do you do about your baggage?

DURHAM I have a saddle-bag with me, and the rest goes to await me at my next stopping-place. But now, sir, before we talk further, may I know the name of those to whom I am so much indebted for their kind hospitality to a complete stranger?

LARRY Burklynch is our name, sir; we come by it from two old Irish families. One of our ancestors, nearly four hundred years ago, was the famous Judge Lynch, whom you will surely have heard of?

DURHAM Only the name. Has it any connection with Lynch Law?

LARRY Aye. To be sure it has. You shall hear the story of it presently. . . . These are my three brothers — Jonathan, Brian and Rory. Jonathan, as you can see, is in the Church, and is now Chaplain to Lord Kenealy at his great house which is ten miles from here: he's just come over for a day or two.

DURHAM Now that is a coincidence; for it was with the intention of paying a call upon his lordship that I came by this road, and missed my way.

LARRY Ah, now that's very convenient and fortunate. He can take you there tomorrow when he goes back to his duties. Now come and sit down.

DURHAM So you are Lord Kenealy's chaplain, sir. Does that give you much to do?

JONATHAN I am also tutor to his son and heir, sir: the rising hope of the family, now sixteen; and a big handful he is.

DURHAM And you teach him — what?

JONATHAN Oh well, just reading and history, and a little Latin.

DURHAM Then you know Latin yourself?

JONATHAN I was taught some; but it hasn't stayed with me. I get most of it from the book, and pass it on to him — enough for what's expected of a gentleman these days.

BRIAN And now that you've heard our names, sir, may we know yours?

DURHAM John Durham, at your service, gentlemen; as some day, I hope, I may be.

LARRY A good name. And you are English?

DURHAM I am English.

LARRY Well, that you can't help, though we'd like you better to be Irish. To be an Irishman is something to be proud of, even though you've only the shoes you stand in, and your honour. You must have honour to be a true Irishman.

DURHAM A good sentiment, sir; but I would say the same for a true Englishman.

RORY And you are not married, maybe?

DURHAM No, I am — not married.

RORY Neither are we, any of us: we are young for it yet, like yourself. It suits better for a man to be free awhile, and marry later.

DURHAM That's as may be. But perhaps I am not quite so young as you think; for I have been married, but am now a widower.

43

RORY You are a widower? Now that's interesting, for I would not have guessed it. Now how long since was that?

DURHAM Just three years ago.

RORY And how came it about — may I ask?

DURHAM Very unfortunately: my wife died in childbed.

LARRY You don't say! Now I call that a contradiction in terms, for a woman to die bringing a life into the world.

DURHAM That it seemed to me cruelly wrong, I need hardly say.

RORY Well, well! It's a sad thing to be a widower. You will not want to be that for long, I'm thinking. . . . Ah, here comes my sister.

(*Enter* HONOR)

LARRY Honor, this is the gentleman whom it is our good fortune to have as our guest for the night —Mr. John Durham; Mr. Durham, this is our sister, Miss Burklynch.

HONOR You are welcome, Mr. Durham. It's late; but we'll do the best we can for you.

DURHAM I am sorry, Miss Burklynch, to be giving so much trouble through my acceptance of your kindness.

HONOR Ah! it's no trouble. It only happens there's so little in the house; and the only bed we can offer you will need some airing.

(*As she speaks she arranges the things which* RORY *has left in disorder*)

Jonathan, come to the table, and do the carving. Now will you start on this, Mr. Durham? And I bring you something nice and hot presently, that you shall like better. Now you take your seat, sir, and begin. And you will excuse me having to go now, so that you won't have to wait for what next I'll be bringing you.

DURHAM Your very grateful and obedient servant, ma'am.

(*She starts to go.* LARRY *calls after her*)

LARRY And the hot water for the whisky, Honor.

HONOR It's all ready. Let one of you come for it.

LARRY You go, Rory.

(*She goes, and* RORY *follows her out.* MR. DUR-HAM *has sat down:* JONATHAN *carves for him*)

Now that's our sister, Honor, Mr. Durham. She's a wonderful one for managing the house, and the making, and the mending, and everything. And a great loss to us she'd be, if she were ever to marry. Oh! there's many have offered from all round the county; but she's turned them all down — so far. That ham, now, is of her own curing. It's good, isn't it?

DURHAM Excellent.

(RORY *returns with the hot water*)

LARRY Ah, and here's the hot water for the whisky.

(LARRY *proceeds to pour out the whisky*)

You'll not want much water to it, maybe? Just enough to warm it. I'll be careful.

DURHAM I would like it quite hot, please.

(LARRY *pours slowly and tentatively*)

More — more, please.

LARRY Ah, then, I'll have to spoil it for you! (*He pours more*) Say when.

DURHAM Thank you.

LARRY You are an abstemious man, Mr. Durham. Here in Ireland we prefer that the whisky should do the heating, not the water. Now you just eat, and finish that off quick, so that I can give you another. And while you are at it, you can just leave us to do the talking. I was telling you that, on one side of the family, we are the descendants of Judge Lynch; a man with a great sense of honour, he was, and Justice of the Peace for the County, in the reign of Henry the seventh.

DURHAM So long ago as that? And what have you to tell about him?

LARRY It's a famous story in these parts. He hanged his son for killing a man; that being the law, and he being County Justice sworn to administer it impartially.

DURHAM And his son was a murderer?

LARRY In a manner of speaking, yes — legally; but truly — no. He just killed the man that had done a dishonour to the woman that he was for marrying. And all the people so loved him, and approved of him for doing it, that no one would give a hand to it. So his father hanged him himself. They were both men of honour, you see; 'twas in the family: each was right, and did each his duty.

DURHAM What happened after?

LARRY Oh, they gave him a grand funeral, which was all they could do to show the respect they had for him. The father — he shut himself up, and died of a broken heart. No one ever saw him again. It makes a fine story; and it's been in the family ever since.

DURHAM The story?

LARRY The sense of honour: and it runs strong in the family still, I would be telling you. 'Twas a great example for all of us.

DURHAM Yes, indeed; but a most sad story.

LARRY 'Twould have been sadder, if neither had done what he did do. They were right, both of them.

DURHAM That is an interesting point of view. Yes, I suppose each did what he thought was right.

LARRY Aye: the one standing for the law, and the

46

other against it. There's been a lot of that in Ireland — hundreds of years: most of Irish history comes into that — it's either the one or the other.

JONATHAN May I be giving you a bit more, Mr. Durham?

DURHAM No more, thank you.

> (HONOR *comes in with the scrambled egg, which she sets down before him*)

HONOR I hope I've not kept you waiting, Mr. Durham.

DURHAM You have not, ma'am. But this is far more than I shall need. I have already done excellently.

HONOR Ah! now just you eat it! And I'll tell you something that you wouldn't guess maybe: those are turkey's eggs, those are. And you will excuse me again, sir, for not staying. There's still things I must see to.

DURHAM (*half rising*) Your very grateful servant, ma'am.

> (*She goes.* DURHAM *starts eating*)

Ah. Very good indeed, excellent! So you breed turkeys?

LARRY We do. They're silly birds; but they lay good eggs.

DURHAM Silly?

LARRY Aye. D'you know that, if they don't go up to roost by sunset, they can't see to do it when it gets dark; and have to stay down. And when they are up, a fox has only got to come and look at them long enough, and they drop into his mouth, so frightened they are! Aye, they are that foolish; but they are good for eating, and their eggs too.

DURHAM A very curious bit of natural history that. I've never heard it before.

LARRY It's true enough. Well, we'd lost several of

them that way; and then, one day we played Mr. Fox a trick. After they'd gone up to roost, we hung a net under them, too high up for him to reach; and when the fox came along and started to make them fall for him, the usual way, they all dropped into the net one by one, where he couldn't reach. And next morning there they were all safe, but very sorry for themselves, after the bad night they'd had. And there, would you believe it? — just where the fox had stood, the ground was all wet as if it had been raining — his mouth had so watered for the meal he couldn't get to. And ever since that — for a fox has a good opinion of himself — to be made a fool of has so hurt his feelings that he's never come near them again.

DURHAM A remarkable story; and you've told it well, sir.

BRIAN Aye. Larry's the great talker; he talks all our heads off, there's no stopping him. But what he's been telling you is true — in a measure.

JONATHAN I'm wondering, Mr. Durham, what are your politics?

DURHAM My politics? Well, perhaps here it would be safer to say that, for the present, I've left them behind me in England; the politics of North Ireland and England don't always agree.

JONATHAN They do not. I'm afraid that means, sir, that you approve of Catholic Emancipation.

DURHAM I think that it had become necessary.

JONATHAN You are not a Papist, I'm hoping?

DURHAM No; my church is the Church of England, as by law established; the same, in its tenets, as yours, sir, though under another name.

JONATHAN Aye; but there are differences. And as regards Papists, we know better what we are up against than you do away over in England.

DURHAM In what way, sir?

48

JONATHAN You mustn't forget that in other parts of Ireland (though not here, thank God) they are the great majority. And now that they've got the vote, there's sure to be trouble, if they think that they are going to get laws made to their own liking. They've been given the vote to keep them quiet; but they must be careful how they use it.

DURHAM Well, sir, we can only hope that the trouble won't ever be so bad again as it has been in the past. But as I said just now, in coming to Ireland I have left my English politics behind me. And now my thanks to all of you — more especially to my kind hostess — for this very good dinner. This egg-dish is excellent.

(*As he speaks, he finishes his glass of whisky*)

LARRY When you have finished that, will you not try a bit of cheese? It's of our own making.

DURHAM No: I thank you.

LARRY Ah! but before you go on you must have some more whisky.

(*He starts to pour it;* DURHAM *makes a gesture to stop him*)

DURHAM Thank you! Thank you! No *more*, please!

LARRY Ah! now, have I offended you? I said a rude thing then. I apologize.

DURHAM Rude? In what way?

LARRY I said 'Will you have *more*?' You should never say 'more' to a man when you are offering him the whisky. You should leave 'more' out — making believe that he's had none so far. It's the polite way we have in Ireland: maybe, in England, you don't take the same precaution not to give offence.

DURHAM This is the first time I've heard of such a

polite rule — a very hospitable one, and characteristic of your Irish kindness.

LARRY Aye: we Irish are kind to each other, except where religion comes in.

DURHAM It's a pity that religion should cause unkindness, amongst those who profess it — more especially the Christian religion. It seems to me rather a contradiction of what should be.

JONATHAN Are you a religious man, yourself, sir?

DURHAM I make no such claim; but I try to live in charity not only with my neighbour, but with all men. It makes life so much pleasanter.

JONATHAN It does. But in my profession one that has his religious convictions must set a stiff face against all false doctrine — especially what comes from Rome.

BRIAN If Jonathan is going to talk to you about his religious convictions, Mr. Durham, it's an unexplored country, I'm thinking, that he'll be taking you into.

(*He gets up, and moves toward the door*)

Larry, I want you. You'll excuse us, Mr. Durham. We've a matter to talk over which must be settled tonight. (*Then, aside to* RORY) Rory, fill up his glass for him.

(BRIAN *and* LARRY *go out*)

JONATHAN And now that you've finished, will you not come up to the fire, Mr. Durham. Do you not smoke?

DURHAM I do not. I never took to it.

RORY Now that is a deprivation for any man — not to smoke. Ah, then, you must make up for it, in other ways. I'll fill up your glass, and bring it over just for you to have by you.

(*He starts pouring a good half-tumbler*)

50

DURHAM No, indeed! No more, thank you! I have already had quite as much as is good for me.

RORY Ah, but see! I've already poured it out for you. I'll just set it there, (*he brings it over and places it at* DURHAM's *elbow*) and you'll think better about it later. It's good whisky; and it hasn't paid duty: we see to that. I wouldn't wonder but, in Ireland, there's more whisky drunk that hasn't paid duty than that has.

DURHAM Do you feel no obligation, then, to provide a sufficient revenue for the carrying on of your country's government?

RORY We do not; and for a good reason why. It's a foreign government we have here now. Since the Act of Union has taken from us our own parliament, and was passed over our heads without our wanting it, it's the English vote that decides our laws for us now. So we don't feel the same obligation to them that you do. And smuggling is a very interesting industry in these parts, and needs a lot of skill to make it profitable, and also a kind neighbourly understanding between the poor and the gentry that it shan't be interfered with.

DURHAM Well, you and your brothers are certainly teaching me a good deal about Ireland that I didn't know before. It's a fresh view of things I'm getting.

JONATHAN So this is your first visit to Ireland, Mr. Durham.

DURHAM It is.

JONATHAN But you already know Lord Kenealy, I take it, as you are calling on him?

DURHAM I can hardly say I know him. We have corresponded. He has a living in his gift, and I have been informed privately that he wishes to sell the gift of it. (*This is a shock for* JONATHAN)

JONATHAN Indeed? This is the first I've heard of it.

DURHAM I gather that — the present incumbent being old and infirm — it is likely soon to fall vacant. And having in England a friend to whom I am much indebted, who is a clergyman, and who would like to live in Ireland, I am proposing to buy the gift of the living and present it to him.

JONATHAN (*with an eye to number one*) I do not think, sir, an English clergyman would find himself at all at home in Ireland: no, sir. It would be a great mistake for him. I hope you don't mind me telling you.

DURHAM He is of Irish extraction, sir; and still has relatives living in this country. Otherwise I should be inclined to agree with you.

JONATHAN I am surprised, sir, that I should have received this information from a stranger, and that Lord Kenealy has said nothing to me about it. I thought I was more in his lordship's confidence.

DURHAM Oh, well, nothing has been settled about it yet. Lord Kenealy may not accept my offer.

(*Enter* HONOR)

HONOR Well, Mr. Durham, have you made a good meal? Have you had enough? And have you liked it?

DURHAM I've indeed, ma'am. Before you came in I had already said my grace for a very excellent meal; and I say it again. For what I have received the Lord — with you helping him — has made me truly thankful.

(HONOR *starts clearing the table*)

HONOR And what would you be liking for your breakfast in the morning, Mr. Durham?

DURHAM Whatever you give me, ma'am, I am sure that I shall enjoy.

HONOR Well, you can have bacon and eggs, the same as you do in England; and porridge as well, if you like. And would you prefer tea or coffee?

DURHAM I would prefer coffee, ma'am; if I may.

HONOR And what time would you like to be called in the morning?

DURHAM Not too late, please; for I must be getting on my way: losing it tonight has delayed me.

JONATHAN It'll be no use, Mr. Durham, for you to be too early, if you are coming to pay a call on my Lord Kenealy. You'll not find him out of his bed before noon. And it'll take us only a little more than an hour to get there. . . . Nine o'clock will be soon enough, Honor.

HONOR Very well. And I'll hope to see more of you in the morning before you go, Mr. Durham. And your room is ready for you, whenever you like to go, except that I must go up first and warm the bed. So I'll say good night to you, and I hope you'll sleep well.

DURHAM Good night, ma'am; I am quite sure that I shall. Your grateful servant.

(HONOR *goes*)

JONATHAN Are you ready for your bed now?

DURHAM I am, indeed, sir.

JONATHAN Did I not hear you say to my brother that you'd like to go and have a look at your horse before you went?

DURHAM You did. May I? He's a nervous fellow; and his fall has upset him. I'd like to see that he has settled down.

JONATHAN I'll take you over to the stables now, then. (*They start to go out*) There's another horse there, did you see? It's one that Lord Kenealy lets me have when I come over for the night, now and again.

(*As they go out they meet* LARRY *and* BRIAN *coming back*)

Larry, I'm taking Mr. Durham over to the stables to see his horse before he goes to bed.

53

LARRY Aye: do.

JONATHAN This way, sir. (*They go out*)

BRIAN Rory, I've been talking to Larry about it.

RORY About what?

BRIAN About how I've thought of a way for getting Honor married to Mr. Durham.

RORY You haven't told me anything yet, beyond a word or two.

BRIAN I've told Larry more, and he thinks well of it.

RORY And what is it?

BRIAN Oh, it's very simple, once we've got over the preliminaries, which'll take a little doing, maybe. Now supposing we were to find the gentleman with our sister Honor in compromising circumstances — what would we have to do about it but to make him marry her?

RORY And if he refused, what then?

BRIAN Why, as men of honour we would have to call him out. And what chance would he have of getting off alive, after having to fight the three of us.

RORY The three?

BRIAN Aye: if he got the better of the first, he'd have to take on the two others: Jonathan, because of his cloth, being disqualified — unfortunately.

LARRY But, Brian, there's just one difficulty, I see.

BRIAN What?

LARRY If he *were* to promise, how would we be sure he'd keep it, once he was let free. For Englishmen have not the same sense of honour that we Irish have for keeping our word.

BRIAN We wouldn't let him get away free, till he'd married her.

LARRY And how would you manage that?

BRIAN Oh, Larry, you are a big fool! Haven't we got Jonathan here? And what use of a brother in Holy orders, if he can't marry a woman on the spot, to save her honour?

54

LARRY That would be very irregular.

BRIAN Let it be!

LARRY And what would the Bishop say? It might make Jonathan miss getting the family living.

BRIAN Och! Who'd know? Do you think Mr. Durham would let anyone hear of his having had anything so humiliating happen to him as that?

(The sound of the outer door shutting is heard)

Ah, here they are coming back. Rory, go and keep Honor from going up, till Mr. Durham has got to his room.

RORY How will I do it?

BRIAN Oh, well, if need be, you must cut three of your fingers, and get her to bind them up for you. It's important, mind! And be quick about it! (RORY *goes*)

(JONATHAN and DURHAM come in again)

LARRY Well? is he all right?

DURHAM He is; he looks quite settled and comfortable now.

BRIAN Mr. Durham, I'll be taking your bag up to your room, and see if it's ready for you. I'll call down for you if it is.

DURHAM Thank you.

(BRIAN goes)

LARRY My sister has been getting it ready for you; you won't have to wait long. But, Mr. Durham, here! You are forgetting! You are leaving your nightcap behind you.

DURHAM My nightcap?

LARRY Aye, this. (*He takes up the half-glass of whisky*)

DURHAM But, my dear sir, I don't want it. Your brother poured it out before I could prevent him.

LARRY But sure, you won't let that stand in the way; when it's there looking at you, and asking to be drunk.

DURHAM Asking *me* to be drunk, is what might be the result, I'm afraid.

LARRY Ah, no! That's not possible on so little; and when you are going straight to your bed, what does it matter? Now you'll not be disappointing us. In Ireland we don't think better of a man for going to bed sober.

DURHAM Sober, I shall not be when I've taken this; but I don't like to disoblige you! To your good health, sir! (*He drinks*)

LARRY Ah! now you'll have a good night, and sleep well.

(BRIAN's *voice from above:* 'Larry!')

There's Brian, calling for us. Come on, Mr. Durham.

(DURHAM, *while* LARRY's *eye is off him for a moment, has set down the glass unfinished*)

DURHAM (*to* JONATHAN) Good night, sir.
JONATHAN Good night, Mr. Durham.

(*They go*)

Oh, there! and he hasn't finished it! Well! Well! It shan't be wasted.

(*He finishes it*)

Now that's a sad bit of news he's given me: a very sad bit of news. Whatever will I do about it?

(*He stands thinking. The clock strikes eleven. The* CURTAIN *closes slowly and thoughtfully*)

ACT III

SCENE I

ACT III

SCENE I

The same scene as in Act I — the bedroom in which JAMES
BURKLYNCH *died about a year ago.*

*The furniture has been rearranged; the curtains are
drawn, and on the dressing-table are two candles.*

BRIAN, *carrying a light, puts the saddle-bag down on a
chair, and proceeds to light the two candles. He then goes
to the door, takes out the key, reverses it into the outside of
the lock, and tries it to see that it works.*

BRIAN So, that's all right.

> (*Halfway through the door he stands to listen and
> then calls*)

Larry! . . . . Larry! Where are you?

LARRY All right, Brian. We're coming.

> (*Steps are heard on the stairs.* BRIAN *goes out to
> meet them*)

BRIAN Everything's ready for you. Good night, Mr.
Durham; and pleasant dreams to you!

> (LARRY *enters, followed by* DURHAM)

LARRY You'll be all right here, Mr. Durham. This
is the best bed in the house, and as good a one as you
could wish. My father died on it; and it helped him
very comfortably to his end. He did not take long, nor
have any difficulty over getting through with it, which
is surely the best way when it has to come.

DURHAM Yes; it certainly has its points; though I
hope I shan't die in it tonight.

LARRY Ah! don't have any such thought! We've a

59

strange saying in these parts: 'In the bed that somebody has died in, a marriage follows.'

DURHAM Well, in course of time, I suppose that may happen.

LARRY Ah! but it means the very next time it's slept in. It's a pity, now, we haven't that inducement for you.

DURHAM I shall probably sleep better without it, sir.

LARRY Now that was a good joke, that was! You're right! In here (*he opens a door at the back of the room*) is a powder-closet, which was turned into a dressing-room when wigs went out. They were used, you know, when powdered wigs were the fashion. There's no window; but there's a convenience, and hooks to hang your clothes on.

DURHAM Ah, yes: so I see. (*He starts to unstrap the saddle-bag*)

LARRY I'm sorry we had no one to do your unpacking for you.

DURHAM Oh; but it's no trouble. I travel with so little.

LARRY Then now I'll wish you good night, Mr. Durham; and I hope that you will sleep well.

DURHAM I am sure I shall; for my long day has tired me. Good night, and many thanks for all your kindness.

> (LARRY *goes, leaving the door ajar.* DURHAM *is beginning to unpack, when* HONOR *enters carrying a warming-pan*)

HONOR Oh! your pardon, Mr. Durham; I did not know that you had come up yet. I was coming to warm the bed.

DURHAM That's very kind of you, ma'am.

HONOR (*she prepares to start warming the bed*) Do you like a feather-bed, Mr. Durham? Some don't.

DURHAM I would like anything tonight, ma'am.

HONOR Here, I've put out a dressing-gown for you that was my father's: it's a bit old and worn, but you'll find it comfortable. (*She begins warming the bed*)

DURHAM Really, ma'am, I don't know how to thank you for all your trouble and kindness.

HONOR Ah! it's nothing! To have a visitor come to us is a pleasure that we seldom get the chance of.

DURHAM I feel I have little right to be called a visitor: I am so much more an intruder.

HONOR You are no such thing! You and my brothers have got on well together, seemingly. Yes?

DURHAM They have certainly been very entertaining in their conversation.

HONOR Telling you their stories? Aye, they are full of them. I reckon I've heard most of them — the decent ones, that is. And each time told differently. Have you heard the story of the fox and the turkeys?

DURHAM I have indeed!

HONOR Ah. I thought that one would come, when — being out of hen's eggs till the morning — I gave you turkey's eggs for your supper. How much of it did you think was true?

DURHAM I thought it was a very good story.

HONOR Well, some of it did happen, but not all. Now is there anything else I can get you? A pair of slippers to change into, would be a rest for your feet.

DURHAM Thank you.

HONOR I'll get them.

(*She goes.* DURHAM *sits down and begins to take off his shoes.* BRIAN *comes to the door which has been left ajar, listens, pushes it open and looks in*)

BRIAN (*apprehensively*) Oh! Where is Honor?

DURHAM She has kindly gone to get me a pair of slippers.

BRIAN Ah, you shall have mine. I'll get them for you.

(He goes out and calls for HONOR. *In a few moments* HONOR *returns with the slippers)*

HONOR I've been looking for the best I could find. Brian has just given me these. He's been in here?

DURHAM He has.

(She has left the door ajar. BRIAN *comes, draws it toward him, slowly and softly, and locks it. Meanwhile* HONOR *has put down the slippers, and* DURHAM, *having now taken his shoes off, sits down to put them on)*

HONOR Ah, they fit you all right. And you put out your shoes, and they shall be cleaned for you in the morning. And now, you let me take that coat, sir; for I see that it wants mending, and it shall be ready for you before you go.

(He takes off his coat: she helps him into the dressing-gown)

DURHAM Your kindness, dear lady, overwhelms me.

*(*HONOR, *taking the coat in one hand, and the warming-pan in the other, goes to the door)*

HONOR Not at all. And I wish you a good night, sir, and that you sleep well.

(With her hands full, she tries to open the door, and fails)

Mr. Durham, would you, please, open the door for me? I've my hands full, and it seems to have got caught.

DURHAM *(goes across)* I beg your pardon. Allow me!

(He tries the door, once, twice)

Why — why it's locked!

HONOR The key must have turned itself.

DURHAM But the key is not here. (*He makes a vigorous effort*) We are locked in!

> (HONOR, *after a moment's consideration, says without surprise, and with only a little annoyance:*)

HONOR Now, which of them will have done that?

DURHAM Your brothers?

HONOR Aye; it must be one of them.

DURHAM But — what can he have done it for?

HONOR Oh, just for a joke; he just wants to see how we'll take it.

DURHAM But, ma'am! Such a joke as this, played on a lady, I regard rather as an insult!

HONOR Ah, you mustn't take it too seriously, Mr. Durham. I'm sorry; and I must apologize that such a thing should have happened. They should have known better than to play one of their Irish jokes on an Englishman.

DURHAM But what do you wish me to do, ma'am? Shall I try to force open the door?

HONOR You can't well do that: if it opened outways maybe you could; but it opens this way.

> (DURHAM *takes up the warming-pan*)

DURHAM Perhaps with this, I might be able to knock out one of the panels.

HONOR What! And break not only the door, but the warming-pan, so misusing it? We'd never get it mended, nor the door either. There's few things get mended in this house, unless I do it myself.

DURHAM But do you mean, ma'am, that we are to submit to this treatment without protest?

HONOR Mr. Durham, the more you protest, the more it will please them. The more you thump on the door, and jump on the floor, and the louder you ring

63

the bell, the better they will enjoy themselves. The wisest thing you can do is to do nothing. Treat it as if it didn't matter, and you'll disappoint them.

DURHAM But it *does* matter, ma'am!

HONOR Don't let it! You and I are not afraid of each other. And what does a locked door matter, if we are sensible about it?

DURHAM But how long do you propose, ma'am, that we should stay locked up here together at this time of night?

HONOR How long it will be I cannot say, Mr. Durham. . . . Till they tire of it. And the more we let the matter alone, the sooner they will find that it's not worth going on with.

DURHAM If there were no other way possible, ma'am, I might accept your advice; but — can I not perhaps let myself down, out of the window? For I must try by every means to put an end to this very embarrassing situation.

HONOR Mr. Durham, you'd only break your leg, or kill yourself. And you cannot anyway, for there are bars outside. And, now I think of it, 'twas for a very good reason. Years ago someone in the family went mad, and they kept him here, and put up a grille outside to prevent him killing himself.

DURHAM And of that mad person are you and your brothers the descendants?

HONOR We are not, Mr. Durham, though you might think so. Ah, but it's not madness with them; it's just idle foolishness; and as they never do any real work, they always have to be after some excitement or other. If they haven't that, life means nothing to them.

DURHAM And this, that they are doing to us now, is an instance?

HONOR I shouldn't wonder. They've just done it for a game, or for a bet maybe.

DURHAM Not in the best taste, I must say.

HONOR Oh, they've no taste whatever, not one of them. And a piece of foolishness like this — they never think how it may strike an Englishman. Now, Mr. Durham, sit down and make yourself comfortable; and meanwhile, till they come, I'll be mending your coat for you; for it happens I've got my work-bag with me. Just before I came up, Rory wanted to have me sew on some buttons for him, said he couldn't wait till the morning. Just think of it; selfish, helpless creatures they are! But I believe they are fond of me — in a way.

DURHAM You must have had a trying time with so many to manage.

HONOR Well, of course, a family of grown men with the minds of children — and all gone a bit wild, so they can't get themselves respectably married, is bound to be a trouble. I suppose it's having the mother in me that makes me put up with them; but they haven't broken my back yet, nor my heart either.

DURHAM You are fond of them?

HONOR I am. When they are well-behaved (which isn't often), I've a liking for them. You can't get away from being one of a family — not in Ireland. I've learned patience. But I won't deny that they are a sad trial to me sometimes. Aye, and they killed their old father; two of them did that.

DURHAM Killed their father!

HONOR They did: started shooting at a target for a wager while he was dying; would you believe it? And the poor old man's rage, when he heard them at it, killed him.

DURHAM I had a very different story about his death from one of them — only just now.

HONOR You would. You'd never get a true story from any of them, while he could invent a better.

DURHAM Have they always been like this?

HONOR As long as I can remember. Oh, they will do anything that comes into their heads for amusement. Do you know that one day they tied a sheep and a pig together by the tail, just to see which would pull the other the further. And because they didn't pull hard enough, they set the dogs on them; and, of course, that frightened them; and trying to break away, the pig's tail came off. And they thought that was amusing. There you have them!

DURHAM How did they get their education? Did they have any?

HONOR Oh, after they had just learned to read and write they educated themselves their own way; and it wasn't a good way. When they should have gone to school, their father got them a tutor — of a sort; but he would not stay. One day after he had punished them for something, they put a snake in his bed. Would you believe it?

DURHAM I thought there were no snakes in Ireland.

HONOR Oh! that's just a tale. 'Twas of the harmless kind though; but the poor man didn't know that; and it so frightened him out of his wits, that he left the next morning.

DURHAM But was your brother, Mr. Jonathan, like the rest of them? If so, how came he to enter the Church?

HONOR Oh, there was no great difference while they were just boys together, but he has more sense about him now. He is a calculating character, he is, now that he's grown up. Why he went into the Church was only because there's a living in the gift of Lord Kenealy; and we being relatives, though distant ones, he thought he might get it.

DURHAM (*for whom this has an interest*) And is Lord Kenealy likely to give it him?

HONOR I shouldn't wonder. When he went to be

66

chaplain to his lordship, 'twas half-promised him, if no one else came along who had a better claim. They get on well together; and Jonathan is careful always to please him.

DURHAM What you tell me interests me very much. But, for that calling, your brother must have had more education than the rest.

HONOR He did. He went to Dublin University, and learned just enough of what was necessary; but no more — you may be sure of that. And by now he'll have forgotten most of it.

DURHAM And what education were *you* able to get, Miss Honor: if that is not a rude question?

HONOR My mother taught me what she could. I can read and write, and I can spell after a fashion. But it's little writing I have to do; and the few books we have here in the house — mostly about horses and dogs — I've no time for reading — only my Bible, which my mother made me read every day; and I do still. And beautiful things there are in it, though I don't believe all of them.

DURHAM And may I ask, Miss Honor, whether you are intending to stay here, and spend the rest of your life, doing for your brothers everything that they won't trouble to do for themselves?

HONOR No: I've made up my mind now. I'm going to look for a situation.

DURHAM A situation? Of what kind?

HONOR To be housekeeper to some good man that needs it.

DURHAM Whoever gets you for his housekeeper, will be a very lucky man, Miss Honor.

HONOR It's kind of you to say it. But now will you tell me something about yourself, Mr. Durham. What's brought you to Ireland?

DURHAM Loneliness — mainly.

67

HONOR Then you have friends in this country?

DURHAM None. My loneliness goes with me. Change of air, change of scene, and separation from a past which I have little wish to dwell on, but find it difficult to break with, are the needs which chiefly brought me.

HONOR You are not married?

DURHAM No, not now. My wife died three years ago.

HONOR Ah! that's a sad thing to have happened to one as young as I take you to be. And you have no family?

DURHAM I have a little son just three years old. His mother died when he was born.

HONOR Ah! poor soul! Had you been married long?

DURHAM Less than two years. She was very young: too young, as it turned out; for, I suppose, had she been a few years older she might not have died.

HONOR Oh! You don't say! This is a sad story you are telling me!

DURHAM I don't usually tell it — indeed, I have never told it fully to anyone. But I will to you, if you care to hear it.

HONOR Why, of course, Mr. Durham; if you feel like trusting me with it. And maybe, it's keeping it too much to yourself has been bad for you.

DURHAM Maybe.

HONOR What was the matter?

DURHAM She did not wish to have a child. She had a great fear of it; but, being married, she accepted what marriage required of her; though not willingly — and died of it. With that on my mind, I find it difficult to forgive myself.

HONOR Oh, but you mustn't look at it like that, my dear sir!

DURHAM Nor did *she* forgive me. When I went in

68

to see her, for the last time, she turned her head away from me. There; I've told you all now.

HONOR God! I'm sorry for you!

DURHAM In time, I suppose, the memory will wear itself down, but never out. It still haunts me: her head turned away.

HONOR But, Mr. Durham, you said that you had a little son. Do you not love him?

DURHAM Terribly; so like his mother that sometimes I can hardly bear to look at him.

HONOR And who is he with? You have someone, kind and sensible, to look after him?

DURHAM No relatives; only servants — old family servants whom I can trust.

HONOR Then, while you are away, how he will be missing you!

DURHAM Yes; but he is still too young for it to matter much to him yet.

HONOR But it's not right, Mr. Durham! A child is never too young but what it needs to have its parents there to look after it; and if it has only the one — all the more is he wanted. Do you not think, then, that you ought to marry again — for his sake as well as your own?

DURHAM After what befell *her*, the thought of marrying again I find difficult. To have caused the death of the woman I loved, puts me off. Suppose that were to happen again?

HONOR But it would not! And look you, Mr. Durham, it is only right that a woman should face the risk of it, like a soldier when he goes to war. It's her share in life-giving it is, for the sake of the world-to-come.

DURHAM The 'world-to-come'?

HONOR Aye: I mean *this* world, and what's going to be made of it by those that come after. And do you think that your poor little lady hasn't forgiven you yet?

69

And that she's still got her face turned away from you in the other world? You believe that she is alive somewhere, don't you? Well, then! What a poor backward mind you have to let itself be fastened down to what's over and done. And do you think she isn't glad that she has left you with a son, that is part of herself, body and soul? Aye, soul too; don't you forget that! It is not only bodies that are born, it's souls too! You go home, and look into your son's eyes, and there you'll see his mother's soul looking out at you — alive still!

DURHAM Miss Honor, how have you learned all this — you, who are not a mother.

HONOR It's only human nature. Every woman has got the mother in her — I more than some, maybe, from having had all those poor foolish boys to look after.

DURHAM Then would *you* like to marry also and have children?

HONOR Aye, if the right man were to come along — which he hasn't yet.

DURHAM When he does, Miss Honor, I hope he will be worthy of you. I wish you well. Oh! I wish you well!

HONOR You said that in a very nice friendly way, Mr. Durham, as if you meant it. We've managed to pass the time very pleasantly together, while we've been waiting. I wonder, have they forgotten us?

DURHAM Forgotten us! Impossible!

HONOR Oh, they can forget anything, if it doesn't interest them, or can be left for someone else to see after. When our father died there was not one of them remembered that a coffin had to be ordered, and a grave to be dug. If I hadn't seen about it, nothing would have been done. Aye! it's either they've forgotten us, or it's just to punish us for not amusing them enough by making a fuss about it.

70

DURHAM But, Miss Honor! do you realize what this means? We cannot allow ourselves to be locked up here together all night.

HONOR If they are foolish enough to do it, how are we to prevent it, Mr. Durham? I would not now at all wish to give them the satisfaction of asking to be let out, if it's that they are waiting for. It's a poor foolish lot they will look when they come to release us, and find the joke's been turned against them, by our just not caring to oblige them.

DURHAM You take the matter very coolly, Miss Honor.

HONOR It's the only sensible way. Of course I'm very much annoyed that they should have done such a thing to you; and I shall have something to say to them about it. But I'm not going to hurt myself being angry with them, till I can pay them back in their own coin, maybe. Unless there's a way of getting through their skins to make them feel it, it's no use. Years ago, I remember, how my father got in a rage with them, and turned them all out — for good and all, he said; and they only slept in the barn and came back to breakfast in the morning. So what was to do about it? And father couldn't keep his anger long enough to hold to his word. So he just let them stay. But it's their breakfast they won't get tomorrow morning, without I give it them; and I shall be making my own conditions about it too, which will not be to their liking. But there! here am I talking, and forgetting how you must be wanting your rest after your long day. For I can see you are tired.

DURHAM I am, now that you remind me. But your conversation has so interested me, that I had almost forgotten it.

HONOR Just now, as you sat there, I saw your head beginning to drop. It's your bed you are ready for. You go to it straightaway now, and get a good sleep.

DURHAM But my dear lady! I cannot go to bed with you here! It would be too embarrassing.

HONOR Why more, lying down, than as you are now?

DURHAM And leave you sitting in that chair, all night, mending my coat for me, while I am taking my selfish, comfortable ease on yonder bed!

HONOR Ah! It's not going to take me all that long, Mr. Durham. And I could not share the bed with you. It would not be right. I'll be quite comfortable here. And it's not reasonable, when I've got the bed ready for you, that you should not occupy it. Now, in there's a dressing-closet; and if you like to go to bed properly, as you would do, were I not here in the way, I would not take it as disrespectful.

DURHAM My dear lady, I could not think of it!

HONOR Ah, well, if it's going to make you feel uncomfortable, don't do it. Just lie down on the bed as you are; and pull the cover over you, to keep yourself warm. It's a foolish situation we've been put into; and I'm only asking you to be sensible about it. Excuse me saying, sir, that if it does not upset me, it should not upset you.

DURHAM Very well, Miss Honor; if I shall so be doing what you really wish me to do?

HONOR If you didn't, I would have to ask you to do it as a favour.

DURHAM In that case, ma'am, I cannot do otherwise. (*He crosses over, takes her hand, and kisses it*) Your very respectful and obedient servant. Good night.

HONOR Good night, Mr. Durham. Sleep well, and don't you worry yourself about me. I'll be all right.

(DURHAM *goes to the bedside, puts off the borrowed slippers, then gets on to the bed, and pulls the coverlet over him.* HONOR *looks on with a benevolent*

72

*eye, till she has seen him settle down: she then com-
poses herself contentedly to continue her mending of
the torn coat. After working for a minute or two,
she suddenly stops, and sits up: a thought has come
to her. She gets up, lays the coat on the chair, and
goes across to the door: she takes hold of the handle,
turns it, and gives a vigorous pull; the latch clicks
loudly, but the door does not yield)*

DURHAM (*starting up*) What was that?

HONOR I was only trying the door, Mr. Durham.
It just struck me that, to make fools of us, they might
have unlocked it without our knowing. But they
haven't. A clever trick to play us, that would have
been, had they thought of it. I'm sorry I disturbed you.

DURHAM No matter, ma'am. I was already almost
asleep. I shan't be long about it.

HONOR Aye: sleep well, then; and you needn't wake
till I call you.

> (*She goes back to the chair, takes up the coat, and
> looks it over. Then, carrying it in her hand, she
> goes over to the dressing-table; puts out one of the
> candles, and takes the other over to the small table
> which stands beside her chair. She resumes her
> sewing. Down below the clock strikes twelve*)

(*To herself softly*) What's that? Twelve o'clock striking.
. . . Ah, well! I suppose they've forgotten us. (*Quite
composedly she goes on with her sewing*)

> *Very slowly the* CURTAIN *closes*

ACT III

SCENE 2

ACT III

SCENE 2

The same scene.

Morning light is beginning to show through the drawn curtains. On the small table by the chair the candle is guttering to its end. In the chair, HONOR sits asleep, with the mended coat drawn up over her for warmth. As she makes a slight movement, the coat slides off her knees down on to the floor. She wakes, and looks about her; then picks up the coat, rises, and goes to lay it across the back of a chair near the bed. She looks toward the bed, and sees that DURHAM is still asleep; she then goes and puts out the guttering candle, and, moving to the window, draws back the curtains: from outside comes the twittering of birds. She takes a few steps toward the bed, then speaks.

HONOR Mr. Durham, it's morning.

(DURHAM *stirs, and wakes, but not quite fully for a moment*)

DURHAM (*confusedly*) Oh, good morning. (*Then, coming to himself with a start*) Where am I?

HONOR You are in your bed, where you've a right to be. Did you have a good night?

DURHAM (*sitting up*) Well, I seem to have done; and ashamed I am to say it — sleeping here comfortably, and you sitting-up in a chair all the night!

HONOR Well, as I told you before, I couldn't share the bed with you; 'twouldn't have been right. I was warm and comfortable; and I liked well being in that old chair which was my father's, and thinking of him.

DURHAM But have you had any sleep?

77

HONOR Yes; when I'd finished the mending of your coat, I was off before I well knew. And I've only just wakened again.

DURHAM Well! This is a strange experience we've had together — Miss Honor.

HONOR Aye, strange you might call it, and unexpected. But it hasn't been so bad, now, has it, as you thought it would be?

DURHAM Indeed, no! I shall have good reason to remember it with more gratitude than I know how to express. To have had the good fortune to come to know — as I have come to know — a woman like you, Miss Honor — so generous and understanding, *and* so sensible — is a rare experience.

HONOR It's good of you to say so. And I'm not all that used to compliments not to feel flattered.

DURHAM (*looking at his watch*) Miss Honor! Do you know what the time is?

HONOR What is it?

DURHAM Nearly eight o'clock. How much longer, do you think, we shall have to wait to be let out?

HONOR Oh, it won't be long now, you may be sure. They will be wanting their breakfast, and expecting me to get it for them. Think of that!

(*She goes and opens the window, and looks out. DURHAM, meanwhile, takes off the dressing-gown, and puts on his waistcoat. He is about to put on his shoes also, when HONOR stops him*)

Ah! don't put on those shoes yet; they shall go down and be cleaned for you. And I'll take your coat and see to have it brushed; for it's got mud on it. . . . Ah! There now!

(*For now comes a loud thump on the door. She stands waiting. More thumps follow*)

78

Yes? You can unlock the door, *and* come in. There's nothing here to keep out for.

> (*The door is unlocked; the four brothers enter;* LARRY *the foremost,* JONATHAN *the last*)

Well, you've had your game with us; and I hope you're ashamed of it.

LARRY It's not to you, Honor, we have to be talking now; it's to this gentleman.

HONOR Indeed! And I should think so! And I hope this gentleman will tell you what he thinks of you. I haven't the gift for it.

LARRY No more words, Honor! You can go.

HONOR I can. But I'm not at your orders, Mr. Larry. . . . Mr. Durham, would you wish me to leave you to settle with these gentlemen?

DURHAM I would rather, ma'am, if you don't mind; for I shall have things to say to them which I would prefer you did not have to hear.

LARRY (*caustically*) Aye! Likely enough you have!

HONOR Very well, Mr. Durham. And I'll have your coat to be brushed, and send it up to you presently. And your breakfast shall be ready for you in half an hour. (*She takes the coat, and goes toward the door*) Rory, bring out Mr. Durham's shoes, and take them down to be cleaned for him.

> (RORY, *offended in his dignity, hesitates*)

Aye! I mean it; or do you expect me to do it?

> (*Thus morally compelled,* RORY *takes up the shoes and stalks out*)

Mr. Durham, don't you spare them anything! The more you let them have it, the better it'll be for them.

> (*Then to the* BROTHERS)

79

And let me tell you this — until you've made your apologies, there'll be no breakfast for any of you.

LARRY Honor, you are wasting words. You will please to leave the room.

HONOR I'm obliged to you for your permission. I will.

> (*She goes, leaving the door open; a few moments later* RORY *returns, and closes it behind him.*
> *The* BROTHERS *stand facing* DURHAM, *with all the assumption they can muster of judicial dignity*)

DURHAM Well, gentlemen, I am waiting for your explanation.

LARRY Indeed, it is rather the other way, Mr. Durham; we are waiting for yours.

DURHAM What have I to explain?

LARRY You have spent the night here alone with our sister. That is a matter which concerns the family honour, for which we are here now to demand satisfaction.

DURHAM It is I, sir, who have the right, and the only right to demand satisfaction. I spent the night here with your sister, because the door was locked on us. What have you to say to that?

LARRY Oh, it was locked, I do not deny; and for a good reason: to give us proof (which we now have) that your intentions toward our sister were not honourable.

DURHAM I must ask you to explain.

LARRY The door was locked, sir, as a very simple way of finding out how long you were intending to be together.

DURHAM 'Intending to be together' — meaning what?

LARRY What does it usually mean, sir, when a man and a woman remain alone together at that time of night? It is a foolish question.

DURHAM May I know, sir, which of you, so suspecting us, insulted your sister and myself by locking the door on us?

BRIAN It was I, Mr. Durham.

DURHAM Then it is from you, sir, that I must ask for an explanation.

BRIAN Why I did so, my brother has already sufficiently explained, sir. But I will tell you exactly how it happened. After we had gone to our rooms for the night, I went to my sister's room to speak to her. She was not there. As I went to look for her — passing this door, I heard voices. You were talking intimately together — very intimately indeed. It was then more than half an hour after you had come up to your room; and there was no reason whatever why my sister should still have been here.

DURHAM That is not true, sir. Miss Burklynch had only been in this room a few minutes when we found ourselves locked in.

BRIAN I am not prepared to argue with you, sir, on a question of time. For you, no doubt, the time passed very quickly: that is understandable; and you did not look at your watch while you were talking so seductively to the lady.

DURHAM (*indignantly*) Sir!

BRIAN No, sir. But would you tell me what was to prevent you from asking to be let out — unless, maybe, you only found yourselves locked in when it was too late for appearances to be saved?

DURHAM We did not *ask* to be let out, sir, because Miss Burklynch gave you the credit — the rather poor credit — of thinking that you had done it for a joke; and that the best thing for us to do was to leave you to discover that the joke had failed of its wished-for effect.

BRIAN Oh! it was no joke! No, indeed!

DURHAM No: I perceive now that it was something much worse — a plot to involve the honour of your sister and your guest — for what reason, I am at a loss to know.

LARRY Ah, well! Of course, you will try to put a good face on the matter. What you say is very ingenious, sir; but too improbable for it to be believed.

DURHAM Then will you, please, ask Miss Burklynch to come back? She will bear me out. You will believe *her* word for it, I presume?

LARRY I would have believed her word about anything until last night. I do not say that I will believe it now. A woman, to defend her honour after she has lost it, will say anything. That is only to be expected.

DURHAM The responsibility for what you call the loss of her honour was your brother's in locking the door, and yours when you became a party to it.

BRIAN Tell me, sir: have you ever before spent a night alone with a woman, without that happening which usually does happen in such circumstances? On your honour, answer that!

DURHAM No. I never have.

BRIAN Then it is only now, when you are discovered, that it becomes the exception?

DURHAM The exception is, sir, that never before have I been placed in such a position as to involve a woman's honour.

BRIAN What is the exception now, sir?

DURHAM That the door was locked on us.

BRIAN And you made no attempt to get it opened.

DURHAM To that, sir, you have already had my answer.

BRIAN And it is no answer. And it does not satisfy us. We are not going to argue with you, sir. You are English, we are Irish; and in these matters we think differently; and if necessary we also act differently.

DURHAM What are you proposing to do, gentlemen?

LARRY We are proposing, sir, to defend the honour of our sister — which is, the family honour — in the way that is usual between gentlemen. You have before you, sir, four brothers of the lady whom you have wronged. You will either marry her before you leave this house, or there will be three of us requiring you to give us satisfaction for the injury that you have done to the family honour.

DURHAM (*stupent*) Marry your sister before I leave this house!

LARRY Yes, sir. Our brother, who is in holy orders, and who cannot, therefore, take the same course in such a matter as we have to, will do you that service. It will be irregular, sir; but the marriage will be valid.

DURHAM But this is preposterous!

LARRY You may call it what you like. It does not remove the fact that we consider it to be necessary.

DURHAM Do I understand that, if I refuse, I am to be called out by all three of you?

LARRY You do, sir.

DURHAM And pray, which of the three encounters is to decide the matter? If I win the first, and also the second — what then?

LARRY In that case, it is the last only that will count.

DURHAM I see. Three to one: the chances will be rather against me.

LARRY You should have thought of that, sir, before committing yourself against a family capable of defending itself to the last man.

DURHAM Except the one who is incapacitated by being in Holy Orders? (*He turns to* JONATHAN) Sir, if I should have the misfortune to kill or disable your three brothers, in this very unequal encounter, will your Reverence tell me what course you would then feel it your duty to take?

JONATHAN I should then appeal, sir, to your sense of honour to repair willingly the damage which you find that you have done to a lady's reputation.

DURHAM A good answer, sir. It rather appeals to me. But it is not very likely to happen. Three against one are heavy odds.

BRIAN You are taking a long time, sir, to give us your answer.

DURHAM You must pardon me if I am. This is a matter which requires a good deal of consideration. Miss Burklynch's wishes will also have to be considered.

LARRY In any such a matter as this, sir, we are our sister's representatives.

DURHAM I should hardly have thought so.

LARRY A woman cannot defend her own honour.

DURHAM No? Sometimes a woman is of so fine a character that her honour is in no danger. I think that is the case with your sister. I do not believe that any right-thinking person, who was told the facts, would have any doubt about *her* honour. She is too well capable of defending it.

BRIAN You are wasting time, sir.

DURHAM Apparently — addressing myself to deaf ears and deaf minds. And by which of you am I first to be held accountable for what you yourselves did to bring about this situation?

LARRY I, sir, being the eldest, shall have that honour.

DURHAM Very well. But there is just one matter to be settled first. I believe that, in affairs of honour, the challenged party has the right to choose the weapon. I choose swords.

(*This causes some embarrassment, even consternation, among the* BROTHERS; *for they are* not *swordsmen*)

LARRY I am sorry we can't oblige you, sir. Here, in

84

Ireland, we do not run to swords. You will have to take what is in the house; we have only pistols. There'll be no choosing for you — except that you may have your choice of the pistols.

DURHAM I have the right to refuse pistols, sir.

LARRY Ah! Are you going to refuse to defend your honour on a point of punctilio, such as that?

DURHAM I am concerned about my honour some-what differently. In defending my honour on this charge, I am also defending your sister's. If, therefore, you kill me (and the odds are that you will), what advantage to her will it be? If I manage to survive, it will make no difference either; for I tell you frankly, gentlemen, that I am not going to allow marriage to be *forced* either upon myself or your sister.

BRIAN Does that mean, sir, that you are refusing to act as a gentleman should act, when his conduct is called in question?

DURHAM No, sir; but since you deny me the weapon which I have the right to choose, I will meet (if need be) all three of you in turn . . . but I shall not shoot.

LARRY Oh! but that would be a most ungentlemanly thing to do! To put us in such a difficulty as that. It is not honourable!

DURHAM Of that, sir, I am my own judge.

JONATHAN Mr. Durham, will you allow me, as one whose profession calls upon him to be a counsellor for peace, to make that appeal to you which I said just now would be my final duty in this matter? Should you not be ready, as a man of honour, to repair willingly the damage which you find that you have done to a lady's reputation?

DURHAM Sir, if the situation in which we were placed last night, by your brother's action, is considered by Miss Burklynch to have done hurt to her honour, I am willing to marry her.

LARRY Oh! then that is all right! And there's no need for more to be said.

DURHAM Pardon me, sir; there is. The decision of the matter is for Miss Burklynch; and she must be free to make it.

LARRY Oh! She shall be free! We will all give her permission to marry you. And how can she wish to do otherwise?

BRIAN ⎱ ⎰You are right, Larry!
RORY ⎰ ⎱Why, of course!

DURHAM Really, gentlemen, your power of self-persuasion amuses me. What you are pleased to call your 'permission', means, I gather, freedom to do your bidding — I would advise you not to be too hopeful.

LARRY Ah! we will see! Rory, go and call Honor.

(RORY *goes, and is heard calling* 'HONOR')

JONATHAN Mr. Durham, I hope you will remember the service which I have tried to do you.

DURHAM I shall, sir. I think you may have helped to clear up a rather foolish situation. The decision of the matter is now about to be placed in the right hands.

(*Enter* HONOR, *followed by* RORY)

LARRY Honor, this is the gentleman you are going to marry.

HONOR (*sharply*) Who says?

DURHAM I certainly did *not* say it, Miss Honor. But it is your brother's version of something I *did* say.

HONOR What is all this about?

BRIAN It is about what happened last night, Honor.

HONOR Well! for that have you not yet apologized?

LARRY It was not for us to apologize, Honor. It was the other way.

HONOR Then was it not for a bad joke that you locked us in?

86

BRIAN It was not.

HONOR Mr. Durham! What have they been saying to you?

DURHAM That our being together all last night was our own choice.

HONOR (*furious*) Ah! Indeed! And what have you said to them — about that!

DURHAM I have said, ma'am, that if you consider my acceptance of the situation, in which we were placed by the locking of the door, has done hurt either to your reputation or your honour, I am willing to marry you.

HONOR But, Mr. Durham, it was my fault! You wanted to break down the door, but I would not let you.

DURHAM That they will not believe.

HONOR They will not *believe*? (*She turns on them*) Oh! What liars you are! So this was no joke; no, it was wickedness — done to this gentleman that was our guest! Oh! how ashamed you have made me! . . . Jonathan, were you in this?

JONATHAN (*uneasily*) No, Honor; I was not.

(*This breach in the solid front comes as an unwelcome surprise to the* BRETHREN)

HONOR But you are in it *now*.

JONATHAN I was told, this morning, Honor, that you and Mr. Durham had spent the night together. I did not know that you had been locked in: had I known, I should not have approved. I trust you will let that stand to my credit, Mr. Durham?

DURHAM (*coldly*) I am glad to know it, sir.

HONOR Which of you was it?

LARRY It was all of us. It was the only way of finding out this gentleman's intentions. It is quite evident that you did not discover that the door was locked till it was too late.

HONOR (*as the matter becomes clear to her*) I see! Yes, now I see. And I tell you this. Here is the ugliest thing you have ever done — any of you. . . . I must see Mr. Durham alone. You will all go out!

LARRY It is not necessary, Honor, that you should see Mr. Durham alone. You had plenty of time alone together last night to make up a story which we do not believe. We see no reason for giving you the opportunity for concocting another.

HONOR You do not? For which last piece of insolence you can take that! (*She deals him a hard slap on the face*)

LARRY (*angrily*) Ach! It's a brazen face you are putting on it! What airs to be sure! But there you are! A woman has no proper sense of honour; and when you defend it for her she does not appreciate it.

JONATHAN Be quiet, Larry! She has the right of it. Come on out!

> (*Hoping that he has done himself another good turn, he ducks his head respectfully, to* MR. DURHAM *as he goes to the door*)

Mr. Durham, I have the honour.

LARRY What are you licking the man's boots for? Come on out yourself!

> (*They go; the last of them slams the door angrily behind them*)

DURHAM (*with caustic amusement*) His lordship's chaplain has become very polite all of a sudden.

HONOR (*intent on the larger matter*) Mr. Durham! Do you know what they have done this for?

DURHAM No.

HONOR To force you to marry me, so that they shall not have to give me my dower.

DURHAM Your dower?

88

HONOR Yes: that they promised their father, and wrote and signed it on the day he died. And now that they have the money, they want to keep it all for themselves. Oh, yes! that is why they have done it!

DURHAM I should not have thought that you needed a dower, Miss Honor, for marriage with any man worthy of your acceptance.

HONOR Ah! but I might. I am thirty; and here in Ireland, unmarried at thirty is to be an old maid.

DURHAM And you wish to marry, Miss Honor?

HONOR I wish to be free to marry — if I choose. Oh! but do not think that it is the dower I am after. I would not have wanted it for myself; only to keep it safe from foolish spending. But now they have done this, they shall pay for it! I am going to have that dower — for the satisfaction of my honour — and yours. (*Suddenly she checks herself*) Mr. Durham! Tell me! What was it made you say you were willing to marry me?

DURHAM Nothing *made* me say it. I was but telling the truth. They had much to say about 'the family honour'; and in defence of it three of them were prepared to call me out.

HONOR (*indignantly derisive*) Ah!

DURHAM With a certain reservation, as to choice of weapons, I accepted: not that their sense of honour concerned me much or little; but yours did. And if you feel that what was forced on us last night has in fact hurt your honour — or endangered your reputation, I *am* your willing servant.

HONOR But it has *not*, Mr. Durham! I would not let it!

DURHAM I did not think you would; you have too much good sense and self-respect to let it do so. . . . But hear me, Miss Honor. It is not about our honour — yours or mine — that I am concerned now, but your happiness. Suppose you do *not* marry, are you going to spend the rest of your life with these brothers of yours — giving yourself to the service of their foolish selfish ways — after what they have done to you?

HONOR No: this has finished it. I am going out to service; to be housekeeper to decent people that need one.

DURHAM I wish I could offer to have you as mine. My little son needs the care and affection of just such a good woman as you. And where could I hope to find a better?

HONOR But, Mr. Durham, I would love to!

DURHAM (*shaking his head*) It wouldn't do, Miss Honor. You call yourself an old maid, but you are only thirty. I am a year younger. You are a lady; we are of the same class. Tongues would wag; there'd be scandal. We couldn't prevent it. Even for the kind service which I so need, I could not risk doing such hurt to your good name.

HONOR (*resignedly*). Ah! well; I'm sorry!

DURHAM So am I. (*He moves away, and stands looking out of the window, then turns to her again*) And now, what is it you wanted to say to me alone?

HONOR Well, first what I have already told you, the reason they had for doing this. And now it is your help which I want to make them pay for it.

DURHAM Anything I can do — you have only to tell me.

HONOR Mr. Durham, you have been good enough to say that if I consider what's happened has done any harm to my honour, you are willing to marry me. I do not; and I don't ask it. But I am going to tell them that there'll be no marrying me to you or any man, till I get my dower. And you are not to say that you are willing to take me without, mind!

DURHAM Very well, Miss Honor; I will refrain even from telling the truth, to oblige you. And to see you extract from them that debt of honour which they most certainly owe you — I shall, indeed, be delighted.

HONOR (*confidently*) Ah, I shall!

(*She goes to the table, and unlocks a drawer*)

See! Here's where I've been keeping safe the paper they signed — only a year ago. I'll be reading it to them presently; maybe they've forgotten the words of it, though 'twas Jonathan himself that took them down. I wonder now what he'll say?

(*She takes out the paper; and then (while* DURHAM *is speaking) pen and ink from another drawer*)

DURHAM Mr. Jonathan will be a valuable help to you, Miss Honor. He has come to know that I was proposing to purchase from Lord Kenealy the living which is in his gift. He is very anxious it should remain in the family.

HONOR (*much amused*) Oh! poor Jonathan! To see the only reason for which he took orders snapt away from him! It'll break his heart!

DURHAM He hopes with my connivance, that it may *not*.

HONOR Ah! So that explains it — why Jonathan has gone back on them. And now they are going to get their lesson. I'll call them in. And mind you, Mr. Durham, this is my business. You leave it to me.

DURHAM I will.

(*She goes to the door, and opening it swiftly, discovers* RORY *with his ear to the keyhole; the others behind him*)

HONOUR Ah! It's there I thought you'd be. Come in all of you!

(*Putting as good a face on the matter as they can, they march in:* JONATHAN, *detaching himself from the others, comes last*)

Aye, you are looking very satisfied with yourselves; but you'll be a sorry lot before I've done with you. . . . Mr. Durham is good enough to say he's willing to marry me. But I'm not willing to marry him without my dower. Now what do you say to that?

LARRY You are in no position, Honor, to ask for a dower, after what happened last night.

HONOR Am I not? Then let me read to you this that you all put your names to, so that your old father might die in peace.

BRIAN I did not sign it, Honor.

HONOR No; but you are going to. . . . Listen here, now! (*She reads*) 'We do hereby promise and confirm that until our sister Honor be married, *as she shall be free to choose*, we will take no share of any moneys that do come to us after our father's demise; and that any dower that may be necessary for our said sister's marriage shall be a first charge on the estate.' . . . What do you say to that?

LARRY That the dower is not necessary. Mr. Durham does not ask for it.

HONOR It is necessary, if I say I won't be married without it. No; I am not willing to marry him nor any other man, till I've made you pay for the dirty game you played on us last night. For which he tells me that three of you were for calling him out, as though 'twas for you to decide the matter! The very idea! And if I say 'no' — which I do — how are you going to kill him for that?

(*There is a pause: the* BROTHERS *look at each other in doubt. This gives* JONATHAN *the opportunity to become spokesman*)

JONATHAN Is it your dower you are asking to have, Honor?

HONOR It is.

92

JONATHAN How much would you make it to be?

HONOR Five hundred pounds.

LARRY (*outraged*) Honor! Where are you pricing yourself, with your damaged reputation?

HONOR Who damaged it? Whichever it was who locked the door on us, and the rest of you that gave your consent to it — that's who did the damage. And are you going to cry it about the county what you did to us, and the reason for it? My reputation is quite safe outside this house, unless you give it away for me — or unless I do, if you drive me to it.

LARRY (*startled*) What do you mean, Honor?

HONOR That if it's my damaged reputation you are throwing in my face, I'll have the full value of it from you: and tell the whole world how you locked me up for the night with a strange man, so as to get a hold on us and have him marry me without my dower!

LARRY Oh! You wouldn't do that, Honor!

HONOR I would! What do I care for my reputation, when it's a set of blackmailers I've got to deal with — which is what you are! Mr. Durham shall go out of this house as free as he came into it; and I'll be as free as him. And to whatever man I choose to marry, I'll bring my dower for the proof of my honour, or to pay for the damage you've done to it — you can take it whichever way you like, Mr. Larry!

JONATHAN (*uneasily hopeful*) You mean, Honor, that if left free, you *are* willing to marry him?

HONOR I've said no such thing. And though he has done me the honour — and a great honour it is — of making the offer, I've not accepted it; so it's no use more talking, unless *you've* something fresh to say, any of you.

JONATHAN Honor, I think you'd better leave us alone together for a while, so we can talk the matter over.

HONOR Very well. And you'd like Mr. Durham to come out too, maybe, so as to be freer to get the words right, of something you've got to say to him?

JONATHAN We would, Honor.

HONOR Well, there's the two things you've got to do — make Brian (who did the locking of the door, if I'm not mistaken) to sign on, with the rest of you, that I get my dower before I've to marry anyone — Here's the paper with your names on it. (*She lays it on the table*) And when you've done that, and come down, you'll make your apologies to Mr. Durham, or it's a poor breakfast you'll get — any of you.

BRIAN (*angrily*) D'you mean I've got to sign away my share, when I didn't ever promise it?

HONOR Yes: it's now you'll sign along with the rest. Your old father, who you killed with your shooting, didn't live long enough to make you, so has left the doing of it to me. (*Then to the others*) What do the rest of you say to that? Am I not right?

JONATHAN ⎫ ⎧You've the right of it, Honor.
LARRY   ⎬ ⎨Aye! Honor's right.
RORY   ⎭ ⎩Yes, Brian, you've got to do it.

HONOR Well, there you are, Brian! It's another three to one you've got *this* time. . . . Mr. Durham, will you come on down; your breakfast is waiting. And your coat and your shoes will be ready for you, now that the maid's come to see after them.

(*She goes to the door, then turns to the others*)

And there's no need to be long over what you've got to do; the sooner you are agreed the better it'll be for you. . . . Mr. Durham.

(DURHAM *crosses; they go out together*. HONOR *closes the door; as she does so, her hand is on the key*)

LARRY Come on, Brian, and sign! Ah, she's been thoughtful; she's put out pen and ink for you, all ready.

BRIAN No, I'll not.

LARRY It's no use your saying no, Brian; there's no getting out of it. She's got her knife into us, and she means it. It's proper blackmail, so it is! For look you! To defend the family honour we were for calling the man out; but if the woman won't have her honour defended, what are you to do about it?

BRIAN Nothing that she tells you.

LARRY But you've heard her say that, if we don't, she'll tell her own story of it, and defame us to the whole county.

BRIAN Ach! It's just talk! She can't do it! Who'd believe her?

JONATHAN I would.

(They all turn on him with astonishment)

LARRY What are you saying, Jonathan?

JONATHAN I said that I believe her.

BRIAN Do you mean you believe her story that nothing at all happened last night?

JONATHAN I do.

LARRY Are you in your senses?

JONATHAN Aye, more than you are in yours, in this matter.

LARRY It's not in human nature.

JONATHAN It's in hers.

LARRY Then she's not human; nor he either.

JONATHAN I've watched them both, Larry; and I'm a judge of character.

LARRY Jonathan! I'm ashamed of you! Going back on us like this.

BRIAN It's not going to make any difference for me. I'll not sign.

JONATHAN You will, Brian, when you've heard me.

95

Now listen. It's very important for all of us that Mr. Durham should marry Honor.

RORY Well, we're with you there!

JONATHAN Aye; but not for such good reasons as I have. Mr. Durham is a gentleman of means, and importance. And he's on his way to buy from Lord Kenealy the gift of the family living. So if he goes from us, that goes with him.

BRIAN How do you know that?

JONATHAN He told me himself, not knowing that I had any interest in the matter.

LARRY Oh! So that's why you've been licking his boots for him. There, then, I forgive you.

JONATHAN There's more to it than that. It concerns all of you. He's of a very generous nature, he is. And having him married to Honor, will mean more to every one of us than the five hundred pounds which we were hoping to share.

LARRY I'm beginning to believe you.

JONATHAN You'd better.

BRIAN But how are you going to make him marry her?

JONATHAN By leaving him free.

LARRY It's a big risk, is that.

JONATHAN It is not. Anyone can see that he's greatly taken with her; and she with him. And if Brian signs, and we give her the dower, she'll be so pleased at having beaten us, that the rest will follow. I'm only telling you.

BRIAN It needs more thinking — telling's not enough.

JONATHAN There's no time for it. We've got to do it now. Are you such fools that you can't see that it's a moral certainty what will come of it? If Honor makes a rich marriage, do you think she'll carry that five hundred pounds away from us, without giving us the benefit of it?

LARRY You are right, Jonathan; she would not. I'm for it. What about you, Rory?

RORY Well, I'm thinking that if Jonathan's right I was right too; for when he knocked at the door last night you all laughed at me for being so hopeful about him. And now you've all come round to it.

JONATHAN And what about you, Brian?

BRIAN I'll sign, on one condition, that of whatever money comes back to us, I have first share.

LARRY Ah, there's the Scotchman again. All right Mac-Brian, you shall have it! Come on then, and sign!

(BRIAN *goes to the table and signs.* LARRY *takes possession of the paper*)

LARRY That's all right. So now we are ready to go down and get our breakfast. And see here! We'll let it all be as if it hadn't happened, and be on as good terms again as we were last night. And a pleasant gentleman he is, to be sure.

JONATHAN There's another thing you've to do though, first.

LARRY What's that?

JONATHAN Apologize.

LARRY What for?

JONATHAN Honor says for your breakfast. But there's more reasons for it than that.

LARRY Apologize, indeed! I'll not. I've never apologized in my life for anything I've done that I'd a right to do. If we let the thing be, as if it hadn't happened, it's the most he can expect of us. We are doing the handsome thing by him, indeed we are! And he should be very grateful.

BRIAN All right, Larry! Leave it! He'll not expect it. 'Tis only Honor talking to frighten us. And if she hasn't got breakfast for us, we'll just get it for ourselves. Come on, all of you!

(He goes to the door, and tries to open it)

Damn! The door is locked! She's locked us in!

LARRY Locked us in, you say?

BRIAN Aye! So as to let him slip away before we can get down to stop him. Oh, Jonathan, you damned fool! See what you've done for us now! *(He charges the door)* Oh! Damn! damn! damn!

(JONATHAN has gone to the window)

JONATHAN It's no good: you're too late. His horse is out there waiting . . . I've saved you from disgracing yourselves.

LARRY Salvation be damned! Here! Out of the way! I'll break it open!

> *(He seizes the warming-pan, and starts beating on the door. The door holds; the warming-pan breaks. With confused shoutings they take up the fire-irons, and beat; but the door does not yield. Finally they take up the fender and use it as a battering-ram. As the* CURTAIN *comes down the door is still holding its own)*

ACT IV

ACT IV

The same scene as Act II.

On a small table by the fire, breakfast has been laid for one; a plate with a cover over it is in the centre; to right and left of it are the usual etceteras. The larger table is laid for four; but there is nothing else upon it except a large home-made loaf, and at one end an old-fashioned coffee-urn. DURHAM, *still in his shirt-sleeves, is standing warming his hands at the fire.* HONOR *comes in, carrying the mended coat.*

HONOR Here is your coat, Mr. Durham. . . . Now, see! Would anyone know where the tear was, without looking for it?

(He goes over to meet her)

DURHAM *(after a cursory inspection)* I don't think any-one would. But *I* shall always look for it, Miss Honor, in remembrance of the many good things you have done for me. Yes, I hope to wear this coat till I die.

HONOR Oh! don't be so foolish! Here! let me help you on with it.

(She holds it out while he gets into it)

Now there's your breakfast waiting for you by the fire. Or, if you'd like better to be out of this wicked house, before any of them come down, here's a packet of sand-wiches I've made for you. And your horse is out there waiting by the porch, all ready to start.

DURHAM Do you want me to run away, Miss Honor?

HONOR It's no running away! You're free to go; you made no promise to stay. And you can't be want-ing to meet any of *them* again — unless it's to collect their apologies.

DURHAM If you don't mind, Miss Honor, I would much rather stay and have that breakfast you've prepared for me.

HONOR Very well, then. Now you've not got to wait for the others; set yourself down and begin.

(*He goes to the table and sits down.* HONOR *takes off the cover*)

It's an English breakfast I've tried to make for you — bacon and eggs, with toast, and coffee. And there's honey too, or marmalade, whichever you like best. Will that do for you?

DURHAM Indeed, here's far more than I shall be able to get through.

HONOR Ah, no! Not with a journey before you. (*She goes to the urn*) And how do you like your coffee? — with milk?

DURHAM Please.

(*She pours out the coffee, and brings it to him*)

HONOR There's sugar by you.

DURHAM Thank you.

HONOR Now start away.

(*She then goes across to the door, and calls*)

Bridget! Bridget! Where are you?

(BRIDGET *appears at the door*)

Have you the gentleman's shoes ready?

BRIDGET Yes, Miss Honor; they're here.

(*She brings them in*)

HONOR Put them to warm by the fire. You don't need to put them on yet, Mr. Durham; it's a cold morning.

(As BRIDGET *goes to the door,* HONOR *follows her, and speaks a little secretively so that* DURHAM *need not hear)*

Bridget, have you put away the ham, and all the other things that I told you?

BRIDGET Yes, Miss Honor.

HONOR *And* locked them up?

BRIDGET Yes, Miss Honor.

HONOR Where is the key?

BRIDGET Here, Miss Honor. *(She gives* HONOR *the key)*

HONOR Then now, you go and get that jug of hot water I told you . . . and be quick about it.

*(*BRIDGET *goes.* HONOR *stands at the door and listens)*

I wonder, now, how long they are going to be before asking to be let out. It's the wrong side of the door *they* are *this* time.

DURHAM In what way 'the wrong side', Miss Honor?

HONOR Did you not see? When we came out I just turned the key on them — so you should be free to go, if you wanted to, without any more trouble they might wish to be making for you.

DURHAM Really, Miss Honor, you have an attractively original way of dealing with these big brothers of yours.

HONOR Oh, well, if one treats them like children (which is what they are) it makes it easier to forgive them.

DURHAM You forgive them for what they did to you last night?

HONOR I do; or I shall, before the day's out. You can't be in the same house together without some sort of kindness and understanding — once a thing's over

103

and done with. It will be harder for them to forgive *me*, I wouldn't wonder, for taking their pride down, as I *am* doing — for their good, mind you.

DURHAM You are a wonderful reader of character, Miss Honor.

HONOR Well, give them the credit for it; they had the training of me. And this, which is the worst thing they've ever done, has taught me something; so I'll let that stand to the good for them, without minding too much what's over. And if they've learned their lesson when they come down, I'll ask you not to be too hard on them; just let it be as if it hadn't happened, which is how they'll be wanting to have it, if you let them.

(BRIDGET *comes in with the jug of hot water*)

BRIDGET Here's the water, Miss Honor.

HONOR Just a minute, Bridget. Mr. Durham, would you like some more coffee, before I make it weak enough to go round?

DURHAM No more, thank you. One cup will be enough for me; and very good coffee it is.

HONOR Which it won't be now. Pour it in, Bridget.

BRIDGET (*as she starts to pour*) How much will I put in?

HONOR All of it.

BRIDGET Oh, Miss Honor! It'll drown it!

HONOR (*ruthlessly*) Drown it; don't spare it!

(*With a murmured protest of* 'Oh, Miss Honor!' BRIDGET *proceeds to drown it*)

That'll do, Bridget.

(BRIDGET *goes*)

Now, Mr. Durham. I want your help. Will you mind taking your orders from me?

DURHAM Anything you tell me to do, Miss Honor, I will do.

HONOR It's important, mind! as part of the lesson I'm giving them. You'll please not to speak to any of them, Mr. Durham, till they've made their apologies.

DURHAM If any of them speak to me that will be rather difficult, Miss Honor.

HONOR Oh, it's fine sweet manners you have, Mr. Durham; and you can be polite to them without words. . . . Ah! Hark now!

(*Upstairs, the battering of the door has begun*)

DURHAM Whatever is that?

HONOR It's just their way of saying they want to be let out. They're in such a temper about it, they can't wait.

(*There comes a loud crash of splitting wood; the door has given way. There is a shout of triumph, followed by a tumultuous rush of feet on the stairs. The door is thrown violently open; LARRY enters. Seeing DURHAM seated comfortably at his breakfast, he calls back to the others*)

LARRY Ha! He's here; he's not gone!

(*The BROTHERS enter; JONATHAN aloof and on his dignity a little after the rest. LARRY, with a magnificent parade of self-assurance, proceeds to stage the desired situation of letting bygones be bygones*)

Good morning, sir! I hope you have had a good night, and have slept well?

(DURHAM, *after an interrogative glance toward* HONOR, *gives a bow of smiling acknowledgment. But* HONOR *has not waited to take command of the situation*)

HONOR Mr. Durham is under orders not to speak to you till he has received your apologies.

LARRY (*loftily*) Ho! Indeed? So a gentleman who is here as our invited guest is not to speak to us. Strange manners that is, to be sure!

HONOR 'Twould have been better if you had remembered he was your guest last night, and not just your prisoner.

LARRY The subject is closed, Honor. We are now all of an agreement: Brian has signed, after the rest of us, that you shall get your dower; so we hope that now you are satisfied.

HONOR Almost; not quite. There's the other thing to come yet. Has not Jonathan been able to make you see good reason for it?

JONATHAN (*stiffly*) I do not think, Honor, that it was necessary for you to play that trick on us.

HONOR No; but I liked doing it. 'Twas a satisfaction to let the rest of you know what it feels like to find yourselves locked in.

JONATHAN That was not my doing, Honor.

HONOR No; but you were in there with the others; so I couldn't make the exception for you I would have liked. I'm sorry, Jonathan.

JONATHAN (*still on his dignity*) I am glad to hear it.

(*Meanwhile* LARRY *has been surveying the empty table*)

LARRY Honor, where is our breakfast?

HONOR It's waiting — as I told you — till you have earned it by proper behaviour. There's bread in front of you, so you don't have to starve. If you want more than that, you know what you've to do.

LARRY Oh, indeed! Is that so? It's a fine idea you have of your duty to the family — their morning of all days!

RORY Aren't you going to say grace for us, Jonathan? — For what we are not allowed to receive, the Lord make us truly thankful.

(DURHAM, *as soon as he has heard the sentence of* '*no breakfast*' *pronounced, has quietly laid down his knife and fork, and remains an amused listener: now, to hide his laughter, he drinks off the last of his coffee, sets the cup down, and wipes his mouth with his table napkin. From a sense of politeness he has now finished. Meanwhile* RORY *has continued to please himself by making the best of the situation with ironic humour*)

Brian, will you be good enough to cut me off a nice big notch from that staff of life which you have in front of you?

(BRIAN *starts carving the loaf*)

BRIAN Will that do for you?

(*He presents it to* RORY *on the point of the knife*)

And you, Jonathan?

JONATHAN (*with a stiff sense of injury in his tone*) If you please.

BRIAN Any for you, Larry?

LARRY (*angrily*) You can help yourself! I'll have my proper breakfast, or I'll not have any!

RORY When a she-wind is blowing, 'tis better to be thankful for small mercies, if you can get them, Larry.

LARRY Honor, where is the porridge?

HONOR There's none been made this morning.

LARRY Where is the ham, then?

HONOR In the cupboard of your apologies.

LARRY (*indignantly*) Do you think we are going to stand this?

HONOR I do.

(LARRY *rises in wrath, and stalks out of the room*)

Any of you wanting coffee?

RORY (*with elaborate politeness*) Yes, please, Miss Honor, if you would be so kind as to let me have a cup — if you can spare it.

(HONOR *proceeds to pour out and pass the coffee while* RORY *goes on talking*)

Now I wonder whether Mr. Durham has ever heard of the Minister that had two graces which he would say, according to what was put before him. When a real big feast was on he would lift up his hands and cry 'Jehovah, great Jehovah, for these thy bountiful gifts we thank thee!' And when there was less to satisfy him, he would say 'For these the least of thy mercies, we thank Thee, O Lord.' Real sincere eloquence, I call that.

JONATHAN Rory, you are talking in very bad taste.

RORY And if I am — what taste can you expect me to have, this morning? Bread, with nothing to it, has no taste at all.

BRIAN (*after tasting it*) This coffee is very weak, Honor.

HONOR It is.

BRIAN And I would like some sugar to it.

HONOR There's no sugar for you, this morning.

BRIAN No sugar! What's become of it?

(LARRY *returns, his wrath by no means appeased*)

LARRY Honor, what have you done with the butter and the cheese, and everything? Where are they?

HONOR They are in the same cupboard along with the ham — and the sugar.

LARRY (*striking the table with his fist*) This is an outrage!

HONOR And a good name for it too, if it outrages you properly — as I hope it does. Mr. Durham, have you done? Have you had enough?

DURHAM I have, Miss Honor.

HONOR I'm sorry I can't offer you any more coffee, now. It's not worth it.

BRIAN It certainly is not. I wouldn't call it coffee.

HONOR Nor would I, either. It's just an apology for coffee. You can take it, or leave it . . . Mr. Durham, if you have finished your breakfast, and if it's not too much a speeding of the parting guest, would you not like to be getting your boots on? They'll be nice and warm by now.

DURHAM Thank you, Miss Honor, if I may, for I ought to be starting soon.

HONOR You've a longish way to go, maybe?

DURHAM Over thirty miles to my next stopping-place for the night. And if my horse has not quite recovered from his fall, I may have to walk most of the way.

HONOR He looked all right when I had him brought out this morning. He's out there waiting for you.

DURHAM If he *is* all right, my thanks are due to your brother, for his kind attendance on him last night.

HONOR Oh, Larry's a good horse-doctor. I'll say that for him.

LARRY (*fiercely resentful*) Thank you, Honor!

(JONATHAN, *who has listened uneasily to the talk about* DURHAM'S *early departure, rises and goes to the door*)

JONATHAN Larry, I want you.

(*He goes out, followed by* LARRY)

HONOR Brian, will you cut me a piece of bread, please.

RORY Ah! Very nice and sociable of you, that is, to be sure! — putting yourself on the same stool of repentance with the rest of us.

HONOR Aye! It's where I have to be, Rory, for the family honour, till we've cleared it. . . . And, Rory, will you remember now, to get that jackdaw's nest out of the chimney of Father's room, so that the next time we have a guest there, we can light a fire for him.

RORY Why to be sure, I will.

HONOR Don't only say it this time; do it.

RORY Does that mean that Mr. Durham will be coming back, may be?

HONOR I wouldn't suppose it's very likely he'll be wanting to come back *here*.

RORY It's a pity! We'd like you to come, Mr. Durham.

(DURHAM *smiles, and gives not so much a bow, as a friendly nod of agreement.* LARRY *comes to the door, and beckons*)

LARRY Brian . . . Rory . . . we want you.

(*They go out, closing the door behind them*)

HONOR Now what are they up to now, I wonder?

DURHAM Finding salvation with your brother Jonathan's assistance, *I* shouldn't wonder. My preparations for immediate departure have made him rather apprehensive.

HONOR What about?

DURHAM My proposed call on Lord Kenealy with a view to my purchase of the family living.

HONOR Ah! Poor Jonathan! . . . Well, now that you've all finished I must start clearing.

(*She goes to the small table*)

Oh, Mr. Durham, but you've not nearly done. You've had no breakfast at all!

DURHAM My dear good lady, I've had plenty.

HONOR Not half what I gave you: Why have you left it?

DURHAM Miss Honor, when you deprived those hungry brothers of yours of their morning meal, I could not very well, as a guest, go on eating under their very eyes.

HONOR Ah! So I've spoilt your breakfast! Was I wrong, then?

DURHAM No, you had a perfect right to punish them for what they did to you last night — in whatever way you pleased.

HONOR They did the same to *you*!

DURHAM Yes; but had I felt so insulted that I could not wish to meet them again, I should have done as you expected, and left this wicked house, as you call it, before they came down. As I preferred to remain, I feel that I am still *their* guest — as well as yours.

HONOR Ah! It's beautiful English manners you have, Mr. Durham. You are teaching me something.

DURHAM Not half so much as you have taught me. It has been a wonderful experience. Thanks to you I am a wiser and a happier man than when I came.

HONOR Oh, it's good to hear you say that. Then it's not all unpleasant memories you'll be taking away with you; though the hospitality was not what it should have been.

DURHAM I shall take with me one memory for which I shall remain eternally grateful — the memory of the bravest and most sensible woman I have ever met.

HONOR And a sensible man *you* were too, Mr. Durham — *and* brave, ready to stand and be shot at by all three of them — which is what they call 'honour'; and a silly notion it is, to be sure! . . . Well, I wonder, shall we ever meet again?

DURHAM I should be very reluctant to go without

that hope. Yours has been a hand of healing: I came here a haunted man — sick in mind, sorrowful over a dead past. That sorrow I still have; but it has become a reasonable sorrow. I feel now that she has forgiven me.

HONOR (*with deep feeling*) That's good! That's good! You'll be glad to see your boy again; and it won't hurt you.

DURHAM Miss Honor, I have something I want to say before I go. If I have not already convinced you that, though three pistols were pointed at my head to make me consent to it, it was of my own free will that I declared myself ready to marry you for the saving of your good name — I ask you to believe it now. If we part here for good, I may be missing the best chance of my life. I will be quite frank with you: I am making no declaration of love at first sight, but of something far better — more real, more sure to last — love at *second sight*. What we have been through together has made me know you more surely than years of mere acquaintance could have done. It is something much more than liking or respect — a deep well-grounded belief — an instinct — that we do understand each other so well that we can without risk — even though we met only some twelve hours ago — join hands and hearts for a life of mutual service and happiness. Just now you spoke of my little son, whose need of a mother's love and care will increase as the years go on. Come and help me to rear that young life to a manhood of usefulness and honour. I ask you to be my wife.

HONOR Well, I will say this: I have never yet met a man I would be less afraid to marry than I would you, when I've got to know you a little better.

DURHAM But you *do* already — just as *I* know *you*, far better than I have ever known man or woman before. That is the truth. Can you not believe it?

HONOR I would like it to be true. But see here, Mr. Durham, you are English, I'm Irish; and we English and Irish, we are that different, we've never really got to *know* each other.

DURHAM No; we never have quite. And why? Because we have never yet met as equals. To so many Englishmen the Irish are an inferior race; and the Irish know it. But between you and me there can be no such foolish thought as that. Let us make ourselves the proof, and show them the better way to understanding each other. Over there my little English son is waiting for his Irish mother. He needs you, and I need you. Will you come?

HONOR I will.

DURHAM Ah! When I said you were a brave woman I wasn't wrong.

HONOR And 'sensible' you said too.

DURHAM Yes, *and* sensible . . .

(*He stands looking at her, and then says, half-quizzically:*)

Honor, your brothers won't think worse of themselves, when we tell them this.

HONOR Why? What do you mean?

DURHAM They will think that their suspicions were right.

HONOR Ah! the poor silly fools! let them! What does it matter?

DURHAM Nothing. May I tell them?

HONOR Why, yes.

DURHAM And that it is to be without waiting? I have one or two engagements I must keep. When I come back in a week's time, will you be ready for me?

HONOR Yes, Mr. Durham, I'll be ready.

DURHAM 'John', *please*.

HONOR Oh, very well — 'John' then. Though it

doesn't come natural saying it, all at once. . . . Ah! here they come. I wonder what news we are going to get from them now.

(*The* BROTHERS *enter with a sort of formal dignity, as if for a ceremony. This time* JONATHAN *is leading them*)

JONATHAN Mr. Durham, my brothers have asked me, in their name, to make their apologies (in which I take my share) for the way they behaved to you last night. And I am to say that, in the unfortunate circumstances in which you found yourself placed with our sister during the night hours, they are quite sure that, in your hands, her honour was safe.

DURHAM I thank you, sir. My thanks also to those for whom you have spoken.

JONATHAN And we hope, Mr. Durham, that the friendly relations in which we found ourselves after your arrival last night, before this unfortunate misunderstanding arose, may now be resumed.

DURHAM I hope that they may be; I have very good reasons for wishing to be on good terms with all the members of your family before I take my departure.

JONATHAN Then, Mr. Durham, if you will be good enough to allow it, on that we will shake hands.

DURHAM Certainly; with pleasure — to our better acquaintance.

(*They advance and shake hands, one by one*)

LARRY And now that our little misunderstanding is over, Mr. Durham, we hope that you will stay with us for a while.

DURHAM Thank you, I am sorry I cannot. I have two appointments which oblige me to go forward without delay. But I hope to be back shortly.

LARRY Ah! now that is good news.

DURHAM Yes. I have news for you. Your sister allows me to tell you that, when I return, I shall be taking her back with me to England — as my wife.

LARRY Oh! but this is a great surprise! Mr. Durham, our congratulations! Oh, but it will break our hearts to lose Honor.

HONOR Aye, just for the day, maybe.

LARRY Honor, you are a very lucky woman.

HONOR I'll take your word for it, Larry, just this once. I don't often.

(*She goes to the door and calls*)

Bridget!

BRIDGET (*from outside*) Yes, Miss Honor?

HONOR Bring up the butter, and the sugar, and the ham. (BRIDGET *enters as she is speaking*) Here! (HONOR *gives her the key*) Boil twelve eggs. (*Then, pointing to the coffee-urn*) Take this down, and make some fresh coffee.

(BRIDGET *takes it and goes*)

Look here, you boys! None of you have washed or shaved this morning. Go and do it while she's getting your breakfast — quick!

(*Three of them go out,* JONATHAN *remains*)

JONATHAN Mr. Durham, will you be coming with me to make your call on Lord Kenealy this morning?

DURHAM No, Mr. Jonathan. I have decided (partly on your advice) not to purchase the gift of that living for my friend. I shall look for some other.

JONATHAN I had hoped that you would, sir. I did not take the liberty of informing you before, that I am myself a candidate for it when it becomes vacant.

DURHAM Then you may be satisfied that I shall no longer be standing in your way.

JONATHAN It was almost promised to me when I

became my Lord Kenealy's chaplain. But he is very forgetful.

DURHAM But surely you may remind him, when the time comes.

JONATHAN I fear that he is in need of money, Mr. Durham, and wishes to sell it.

DURHAM If so, I cannot prevent him. I'm afraid I cannot buy the gift of more than one living at a time, Mr. Jonathan; and my friend in England has the first claim on me.

JONATHAN (*very crestfallen*) Oh, indeed? I am sorry.

HONOR Jonathan, you are not any more clean than the rest of them. Go, and get yourself tidy; and be quick before Bridget brings up the breakfast.

JONATHAN I do not think I will wait, Honor. As Mr. Durham is not coming with me, I will be getting back now at once.

HONOR Well, then, you'd better take these sandwiches with you, which I made for him; for he's had a better breakfast than you have.

JONATHAN Thank you, Honor. Mr. Durham, we shall meet again, under happier circumstances, I hope.

DURHAM Yes, indeed; I hope so.

JONATHAN Honor, am I to have the marrying of you?

HONOR No, Jonathan; you'll have to give me away.

JONATHAN Larry will be wanting to do that.

HONOR I do not want him to; I'd rather have you.

JONATHAN Very well, Honor. Good-bye, Mr. Durham.

DURHAM Good-bye, Mr. Jonathan. Will you give my compliments to Lord Kenealy, and tell him that I shall be writing to him presently.

JONATHAN I will. (*And it is a very depressed* JONATHAN *who takes his departure*)

HONOR Poor Jonathan! You've disappointed him.

DURHAM How could I do otherwise? I could not conscientiously present a 'Cure of Souls' to one who has not got an ounce of the curing of souls in his composition.

HONOR And you say that, after the work of conversion he did this morning, when he brought them all to heel, and made them come and apologize to you?

DURHAM For a very material, not a spiritual reason, I'm afraid, Honor.

HONOR You are hard on him, John; but you are right. He's rather a calculating character, is Jonathan.

DURHAM Yes; he'd make a better business man than a parson. And now, Honor, as I'm in the same case as your brothers, and am in no great hurry to start, may I go up and have a wash and a shave before I go?

HONOR Why, to be sure!

(While she is speaking, BRIDGET *comes in with the ham, the sugar, and the butter, and plates; and starts laying them on the table)*

Bridget shall take you up some hot water, straight away. And you can take your time over it: you won't want to sit and watch the good boys having their breakfast.

DURHAM I think it would be rather amusing. Mr. Larry will be in fine form, I shouldn't wonder. And he has powers of conversation that never tire me.

HONOR They don't? Then you've more patience for him than I have.

(As BRIDGET *is going out, she calls her back)*

Bridget, come here! I want to introduce you to this good gentleman — Mr. John Durham, for you to say a kind word to him. And if, while you are about it, you'll say a kind word for me too — as to my character — I'll be obliged to you. He's come over from England to marry me.

BRIDGET (*her voice quavering*) Oh! Miss Honor! You make me to cry, I'm that glad! — that glad! Oh! but you'll be going away from us to England; and never to see you again will break my heart!

HONOR Yes, Bridget, it's to England I'll be going. And you can come with me if you like. I'd be glad to have you.

BRIDGET No, Miss Honor; I can't well do that, as you must know. There's my mother that's needing me, and my good man waiting to marry me. So here's where I belong.

HONOR You are right, Bridget. But if ever it did so happen that you were free to come — and your man with you — wherever I am, there'll be a home waiting for you, and a welcome. Have you anything to say against that, Mr. Durham — John? If you have, you can say it now.

DURHAM I have not, Honor. My English home is yours; and you can make it as Irish as you like.

BRIDGET (*bursting into tears*) Oh! sir; you are going to be a very happy man!

DURHAM Yes, Miss Bridget, a very happy man, and a very lucky man too.

(*But* BRIDGET *hasn't waited; her feelings are too much for her; she runs out weeping*)

HONOR Poor Bridget! She's the one that will miss me most: bless her kind heart!

CURTAIN

EPILOGUE

EPILOGUE

[For book-publication only: not to be acted unless the Producer specially wishes for it.]

Fifteen years have gone by.

In her English home, in a well-furnished sitting-room, hung with family portraits, HONOR, *now comfortably middle-aged, sits holding up a coat for inspection. Standing before her, in his shirt-sleeves, is her stepson,* RONALD DURHAM, *a handsome well-set-up youth of eighteen. In vigorous good-humoured reproach, she goes for him.*

HONOR Ronny! However did you come to tear your coat like this? It's torn in three places.

RONALD Getting through a bramble-hedge in too much of a hurry, Mother.

HONOR Whatever for did you go through a bramble-hedge in a good coat like this?

RONALD There was a dog worrying a sheep on the other side; and I had to get through to stop it.

HONOR Oh? Then I forgive you. Sit down; I want to have a talk with you.

> (*She gets out her work-things, and starts mending the coat.* RONALD *sits down at her feet, and watches her*)

How are you getting on with my Bridget? I want you to be kind to the poor thing: she's had trouble enough.

RONALD What, Mother?

HONOR Three years ago her good man went over to America to make a home for her, and died there. And she lost both her children. And now her old mother's gone, she's coming to me for good. Have you had any talk with her?

RONALD Yes. At least I've been listening: she did most of the talking; she's got the Irish gift — very descriptive some of it. She told me how sea-sick she'd been coming over. And what made it worse, she said, was that she'd nothing to show for it — she was that empty.

HONOR Ah, and I don't wonder. They've had famine over there for three years now, Ronny; and it has worn her down. She came looking half-starved. And here people aren't caring enough about it. D'you know, your father's going over to see what he can do for them? But what can he do? He can give money, but he can't take over ship-loads of food, which is what they want. And it's what the Government ought to be doing all the time. You English mean well by Ireland, maybe; but you don't mean it much.

RONALD Why do you say 'you English', Mother?

HONOR Because I'm Irish. Doesn't my way of talking tell you that?

RONALD Oh, I'm so used to it, I never notice it, to think it means anything. What's it to tell me?

HONOR That I'm not your own mother.

RONALD I don't know why you should ever have troubled to tell me that, for it never seems true to me. Sometimes I wish you hadn't.

HONOR That wouldn't have been right, Ronny. Make-believe is never so good as the truth. And there's good reason why you should keep a warm corner in your heart for the one that gave her life bringing you into the world.

(RONALD *makes a startled movement*)

Didn't you know that? Has your father never told you?

RONALD No, Mother.

HONOR Ah, it hurts him still; but not like it used to do. It was that, and his telling me of it, brought us together, and gave me the mothering of you. . . . Ah! And that reminds me! D'you know, the first time we ever met, he and I, I sat up half the night, mending his coat for him, like I'm mending yours now. Till five hours before I'd never set eyes on him: next day I'd agreed to marry him. Sounds like a fairy tale, doesn't it? But it's true.

RONALD However did it happen, Mother?

HONOR Oh, my brothers had played an ugly trick on us; and that was what came of it. But I'm not telling you about it. Your father will tell you himself some day, if he wants to. Hasn't Bridget told you anything? She was there at the time?

RONALD No, Mother. Not about that; but she has a lot of queer stories to tell about those uncles of mine.

HONOR They were not your uncles — not proper ones.

RONALD They were your brothers, Mother.

HONOR Oh, well! have 'em if you like!

RONALD They must have been a funny lot.

HONOR Funny? Oh, aye! Three of them — their only thought in life was just to have fun — and make others pay for it. Jonathan was different; but no better, to my thinking.

RONALD Why have you never told me more about them, Mother?

HONOR Because there is so much more I wouldn't want to tell. Why do you want to know?

RONALD Just because they're your brothers, Mother.

HONOR They *were*: but there's only one of them left now — or there isn't. For, from what we've heard, any day may bring the news that Jonathan has gone like the rest.

RONALD There was one Bridget didn't seem to like much, I thought.

HONOR Ah! Larry that was: she'd reason. He was

123

the eldest, and the worst of them. He'd a very bad influence on himself.

RONALD (*laughing*) Mother!

HONOR Ah; he had. He always thought that whatever he wanted to do would be good for him; but it wasn't. So, what with one thing and another — the drink helping — he died of it. Oh! but he'd a strong constitution; it took him twelve years to do it, after I'd left off having the care of them. . . . Brian — he went to America: he never wrote home, so we got no news of him, till word came — five years ago — that he'd gone treasure-hunting with a party away south among the Indians; and none of them ever came back alive. . . . Then there was Rory. Ah! he'd a sweet nature: however much you scolded him, he always took it as a joke. He was the youngest of them, but the first to go — broke his neck over the last jump in a steeplechase, just as he was winning it. His horse came in first; but he wasn't on it. . . . They gave him a grand funeral . . . So now there's only Jonathan.

RONALD Where does he come in? — and you, Mother?

HONOR I was the eldest of all. He came after Larry. He went into the Church to get the family living — but it was sold away from him; so there he was left. And then he did the worst thing for himself that he ever did in all his life. There was a widow, a Roman Catholic (Papist we call it), who'd got money; and he turned Papist to marry her. Think of that! And then he found that, by marrying again, all the money went from her —she'd nothing of her own. There's no doubt she deceived him about it; but maybe she felt justified doing it — to bring him into the true Faith. We've never seen her; we didn't want to; and I fancy Jonathan was a bit ashamed of himself, when he found he'd done it for nothing. He used to write to your father to help

124

him; but never to me. . . . Poor Jonathan! He's been a sad disappointment to himself; for he had a calculating way with him. But twice over — in what mattered to him most — the family living that he missed, and the match that he made for himself — he miscalculated. . . . Well! There you've got the sort of family I came from. Is it to wonder at, that I haven't told you anything about them before? . . . What has Bridget been telling you?

RONALD More about *you* than about them, Mother. She thinks you were a wonder; says you did everything for them — which was why (for ten years or more) you never got married.

HONOR Ah! well; if that's what kept me single till I met your father, 'twas a good thing they did for me. So give them the credit for it.

(BRIDGET *enters, and halts — she is carrying a letter*)

BRIDGET Miss Honor?

HONOR Yes, Bridget; come in. What is it?

BRIDGET Here's a letter for you, with black round it. It'll be the bad news about Mr. Jonathan, I'm thinking.

(HONOR *holds out her hand for it: she opens and reads it*)

HONOR Yes, Bridget; it is so. . . . Ronny, go and find your father, and say I'm wanting him.

(RONALD *goes. She looks again at the enclosure, which is not a letter, only an obituary card*)

BRIDGET Does it say anything for you to know how he got through with his dying, Miss Honor?

HONOR No; it isn't a letter; only just a notice, with his name, and the date — five days ago, that was — and saying that he died in the Faith he'd chosen for himself.

. . . Well, Bridget; so here we both are, with nobody that belonged to us left in the old country now. And you've come to the home that's been waiting for you, where we'll be glad to have you. . . . What do you think of my young brood — and Mr. Ronny?

BRIDGET Oh! you've got lovely children, Miss Honor!

HONOR Yes, Bridget! 'Miss Honor' has got three lovely children to her name; with another, as good as them, that's not a child any more. And I'm not Miss Honor any more, either; though you can call me that if you like!

BRIDGET Oh, I'm sorry, Miss Honor — Mrs. Durham, I mean; but I just can't help it — it comes so natural.

HONOR Well! don't then! Here! will you take this coat of Mr. Ronny's, and go on mending it for him? He'll be wanting it again.

(*As* BRIDGET *goes out,* DURHAM *enters*)

Yes, John; the end has come.

(*She hands him the card; he takes and reads it*)

'Fortified by all the rites of Holy Mother Church.' . . . What does that mean?

DURHAM The ministrations which the Church of Rome provides for those who wish to die well in the Faith to which they belong. All that it means, is that Jonathan also had the benefit of them.

HONOR 'Fortified'? . . . Well! let's hope that this last time he hasn't miscalculated. . . . Poor Jonathan! . . . So now the burden of my family is off your back at last! . . . You were good to them, John.

DURHAM They were your brothers, my dear. Oh, yes: they've been a troublesome lot, first and last — a handful that there was no holding — all going their own foolish ways. But if it hadn't been for them, I shouldn't have got *you*.

HONOR And if I'd known a bit *more* about you than I did at the time — you might *not* have got me at all.

DURHAM What do you mean?

HONOR You, a big county man — a magistrate and all — to be bringing a poor Irish wife among such grand folk with their ladies, and all their airs and graces. I'd have been afraid to come; and good reason too.

DURHAM Why?

HONOR Tell me truly, John, do you not mind that I've stayed Irish?

DURHAM Why on earth should I?

HONOR Wouldn't you have wished me to become more English?

DURHAM How?

HONOR In my talk, for one thing. There's some of them (because of it) think I'm not a lady. They look at me almost as if I were dropping my aitches (which in Ireland we don't). Yet there's many of them can't say their 'G's'; and the letter 'R' never comes out of their mouths properly. But they think that's all right for themselves; while for me to be saying them is all wrong. Times I've been afraid that the children would be catching it off me.

DURHAM Let them! Listen, Honor: I wouldn't have my Irish wife give up one bit of all the Irish that is in her — not for the whole world. It means something. And it's that that is taking me over to Ireland now.

HONOR Thank God for that! . . . John . . . will you take Ronny with you?

DURHAM I hadn't thought of it. Why?

HONOR So as to let him see — what he'll never forget — what starving people look like. Hearing about it, is not the same as seeing. Look famine in the face, and you won't forget it. If all your well-fed English folk over here could only see *that*, they'd care more than they are caring now.

DURHAM Very well. Ronny shall go with me.

HONOR Oh, John! How all the nations and races of the world are divided! And there's only one thing that's going to bring them together.

DURHAM What is that?

HONOR Just what's happened with you and me. . . . I'm Irish; you are English; and we don't wish it to be otherwise, because it makes no difference. How I'd like that Day of Pentecost to come again! If it only could! — I was reading of it to the children from the Bible only yesterday, where it's told in a way that you don't have to believe all of it — not that about the tongues of fire, and the rushing mighty wind, and the rest of it. But for all the fancy telling of it, there's real rock-bottom truth in what happened then. . . . What's it say? How they were all filled with the spirit and began to speak as it gave them utterance. And every man heard them speak in his own language. What's it mean? Just understanding of one another. That's all we want, to get ourselves right, one with another. For all the wrong and wickedness there is in the world — if people would only be understanding and sensible about it, it 'ud all come right.

DURHAM Would it? I wonder.

HONOR Isn't that what happened with you and me, John? They did a wicked ugly thing to us, those brothers of mine, when we first met fifteen years ago. But we were sensible about it: so it all came right.

DURHAM Yes, Honor, it all came right. And the Family Honor came safe into my keeping. And I have her here with me now — never to part.

(*He bends down and kisses her*)

CURTAIN